ADVANCE PRAISE

T0002447

If your teen is out of control, here is hope, solace and wisdom. Best of all, here is real help that will make a difference. You are not alone. The author has been there. With clarity and honesty, Lisa Nichols shares not only what she learned; she also gives practical ways to care for yourself through this difficult journey.

– REV. DAVID MCARTHUR, J.D., author
of *Your Spiritual Heart*

I was immediately struck by the level of caring and sharing presented in this book by Lisa Nichols. It's evident that the author had been through a tough life with an out-of-control teen and sincerely wants to help others who have similar experiences. As I read her book, I could see where these techniques could be applied to other areas of our lives, such as family and spousal relationships. She provides very helpful methods for addressing the stress and guilt that is commonly shared by us all. I would recommend this book to any stressed out mothers, even if your child is not yet a difficult teen.

– TRICIA LINDEN, author of *Until We Meet Again*
and eight additional books

Lisa Nichols writes with a clear voice that is exceptionally instructive while never losing its caring and compassionate tone. With vulnerability, she shares her personal struggles raising an out-of-control teen that lets the reader know that they are not alone in their pain and suffering. She came to the realization, "If I wanted a different experience, I would have to change myself." In her healing and self-growth journey, she discovered a transformational tool that helped her transform the overwhelm, shame, and guilt that had plagued her long after her son became an adult. It is the Emotional Freedom Techniques (EFT), or tapping. Through this book I learned that I needed to tap on ALL aspects of an event - the images, the sounds, tastes, thoughts and beliefs…not just the emotions. I have used her easy to use scripts to clear my own shame and guilt about the way I dealt with my teenage daughter. Lisa has grown from her experience and has great wisdom to share. This book will be tremendously helpful to other parents who feel lost and don't know what to do with their teen.

> – CAROLYN JANSON, MA Secondary Education, teacher, educational consultant, Resilience Coach

Surviving Your Out-of-Control Teen

SURVIVING YOUR
out-of-control teen

A Mom's Guide to Loving Your Child
Through the Difficult Times
While Keeping Your **SANITY INTACT**

Lisa Gay Nichols

NEW YORK

LONDON • NASHVILLE • MELBOURNE • VANCOUVER

Surviving Your Out-of-Control Teen

A Mom's Guide to Loving Your Child Through the Difficult Times While Keeping Your Sanity Intact

Published in New York, New York, by Morgan James Publishing in partnership with Difference Press. Morgan James is a trademark of Morgan James, LLC.
www.MorganJamesPublishing.com

ISBN 9781642797220 paperback
ISBN 9781642797237 eBook
ISBN 9781642797398 audiobook
Library of Congress Control Number: 2019945481

Cover Design by:
Megan Dillon
megan@creativeninjadesigns.com

Interior Design by:
Chris Treccani
www.3dogcreative.net

Morgan James is a proud partner of Habitat for Humanity Peninsula and Greater Williamsburg. Partners in building since 2006.

Get involved today! Visit
MorganJamesPublishing.com/giving-back

For Jason and Sabrina, my biggest teachers
who I love even more than Panda.

And for John, who lived it with me
and still stayed sweet.

I believe our darkest truths can become our beacons of light, and our most painful admissions can become catalysts for change. With every honest look inward comes life-changing awareness.

– Rachel Macy Stafford

TABLE OF CONTENTS

WHY I WROTE THIS BOOK FOR YOU

It's been a few years since I was a mom with an out-of-control teen. But I remember the hardships of those days and wouldn't wish them on any parent.

I felt so unprepared when my son really started spinning out of control. It's not something I ever imagined going through. I had no idea where to start to help him, and I had little ability to discern what would work.

It was a lonely time. It seemed like no other parent was going through what we were going through. It was so disappointing to hear about parents whose teenagers were succeeding at sports, getting good grades, winning awards, having interests that they pursued, or just being polite once in a while. As much as I know that I shouldn't compare my children to others, it was hard not to. I would have been thrilled if my child had "normal" teenager problems!

As I was going through those years, one frustration was all the "expert" advice that did not work. Maybe it works for

xvi | **SURVIVING** YOUR Out-of-Control Teen

other teens, but not our son. We tried and tried, hoping and thinking that he would turn around, until it was almost too late.

After years of trying so many different things, I found one of the best ways I could help my teen was by helping myself. I looked at what was driving my parenting – the stuck emotions and beliefs that kept me from being the parent I'd really like to be.

And that's why this book came into being. In it, I share with you honestly about what the experience was like for me and how I got my relationship with my child back on track. You might think at times that I was a hot mess and even feel sorry for my kids. That's okay – I think that sometimes, too!

I wish I had the advice in this book a long time ago, even before my son was a teenager. I believe what we experienced would not have been as extreme, and we would have gotten through it with less stress and in a shorter amount of time (and less expensively). It's not that I am a perfect parent now, by any means! But my relationship with my son has changed for the better, and I am so grateful that he has come a long, long way from where he was.

I hope this book helps you find the answers that you need.

I hope it helps you make decisions with more ease and more faith about what to do to keep your child safe.

I hope it helps you realize that you don't need to feel guilt, shame, embarrassment, or regret about your child's choices and behavior, no matter what ultimately happens.

I hope it helps to strengthen your relationship with your child.

I hope it makes you feel less alone.

And above all, I hope it helps you find an inner calm and peacefulness as you move through this challenging time.

CHAPTER 1:

It's Never Too Late

I f you are dealing with an out-of-control teen, I really, really feel for you. It's no fun, to say the least!

It is a stressful, unhappy, difficult time that can be heartbreaking and isolating. Remember when your son or daughter was little and sweet and loved you so much? It's hard to believe they are the same person as the furious, argumentative, disrespectful teenager they are now.

Not only do they not recognize the danger they are putting themselves, their families, and their homes in, they don't see that their actions can impact their futures for years to come. The possibility of addiction, pregnancy, serious injury, lost potential – these are all the stuff of nightmares for us parents. Just to get them to graduate high school will be a major win!

1

Even as horrible as it is to be around them, I have great empathy for these teens. Their actions are stemming from a mix of hormones, immaturity, inexperience, feelings they don't know what to do with, and beliefs that don't serve them.

I know you have a lot going on right now, and the last thing you need is one more thing to do. And you certainly don't need any more advice; there's plenty of that coming at you from the school, doctors, family, friends, and even complete strangers. But, as the mom of a former difficult teen, there is something I believe will help you tremendously. And it has nothing to do with your child.

It has to do with looking at yourself and the beliefs that you hold.

It may sound like I'm blaming you for your child's behavior. I'm not. I'm not trying to make you feel guilty, and I'm certainly not taking accountability off of your teen for their actions.

But how you parent and how you react to your teen's behavior is based on the beliefs through which you filter your experiences. These beliefs were probably formed long ago and then were reinforced by how you perceived subsequent events. For example, if, in the guise of wanting you to do your best, your parents criticized everything you did, you would come to believe that nothing you did was ever good enough or that you had to be perfect. From then on, you would ignore anytime someone praised your accomplishments and would only hear when someone criticized you.

That's why you get triggered and end up reacting emotionally and saying or doing things you regret later – despite your intention not to. There were countless times that I swore to myself that I would listen to my children when they brought up a frustration, and within a day, darn if I wouldn't just launch into my own story or defense or start giving advice without hearing them out. I was so wrapped up in a belief that I had to be right that I couldn't hear them – sending them messages that what they had to say wasn't important. I would kick myself for days for once again missing an opportunity to connect with them.

By releasing the beliefs that have been guiding and informing you as a parent, you can change everything. You can change the dynamic of your relationship with your teen. You can change how you feel about yourself and your role in this situation.

Are you feeling guilty, like it's all your fault? Feeling like you need to blame others, such as the school? Feeling ashamed, because you think you've been a terrible parent? All of these feelings are being driven by the beliefs you hold and therefore the meanings you give to what's happening.

You can better help your child if you release the emotional baggage and limiting beliefs that don't serve you. The circumstances didn't develop in a vacuum, and they will stay in place until something changes. And you can be the one to create the change.

The technique that I recommend is called Emotional Freedom Techniques (EFT), or tapping. The reason I recommend it? I have been on my personal healing and self-growth journey for almost two decades, and it's been since I started using tapping on a regular basis that the positive changes about how I feel about life went through the roof! Through tapping, I have gained an amazing sense of openness and calm. I never thought that I could feel so peaceful and have such a clear, neutral view of events in my life. Now when my children bring up a frustration, I don't rush to give advice or defend. I can listen patiently, ask clarifying questions, and give them my attention and care instead of trying to relieve my own uncomfortableness.

Tapping is a simple, easily applied technique that can eliminate emotional intensity around traumatic experiences. It helps you release emotions, fears, and beliefs that keep you stuck. Tapping can literally reprogram the subconscious thoughts and patterns that prevent you from learning new ways of interacting with your child (and everyone else in your life) that talking alone doesn't seem to address.

This is about you

Notice that I haven't said anything about working with your child. As you begin seeing benefits from tapping, I suggest that you not attempt to get your child to try it, especially when you are still new to it. If they ask about it and are willing to try it, I suggest you have them work with someone who is experienced with tapping, such as a practitioner, so that this opportunity to help your child is fully taken advantage of.

Even though you won't be working on your child, you will likely bring about change in them. As you shift your limiting beliefs and stored emotional trauma, you will naturally begin to react to your teen differently. You will be able to better see and honor who they are as their own person. When you change things up and react differently, they will also have to change how they react because they won't be getting the same triggers or the same responses that they expect.

An important note: let go of the outcome. Don't do this work to change your child. Do this work only for yourself, to give yourself more peace of mind and a clearer picture of the situation.

It's not too late to change how you parent. It's not too late to change your relationship with your child. It's not too late to change how you feel about yourself. And tapping can help you get there.

Special notes:

- If you or your child has experienced verbal, physical, or sexual abuse, a major accident or an assault, I urge you to work with a professional therapist or practitioner if you are not already. If you get triggered by doing the tapping exercises in this book, contact a professional therapist or practitioner immediately.
- For parents of adopted children, I know there are concerns over and above those of teens who were not adopted. As you get to know how to use tapping effectively, you can tap on the issues specific to the adoption. My wish for you is that your children know that they are not flawed or unwanted, but are deeply loved.
- If your child has stated that they are queer or gender-fluid and you have a religious objection or do not feel prepared to deal with it, you may wish to speak with a practitioner or therapist specifically about this concern.

Now I'm going to lay it all out there and tell you about my experience with my own out-of-control teen.

CHAPTER 2:

My Story

'm staring at a picture of me and my son that sits on my desk. He's about five, wearing a cap and holding a bat in front of him. I'm kneeling with my arms wrapped around him. I'm smiling brightly; he's looking down to avoid the sun.

How I loved those pinchable cheeks.

There were signs even then of the challenges to come. He got into more trouble than most kindergartners. Our efforts to get him into team sports – soccer and t-ball – failed epically. His teachers would seat him away from other students so he couldn't continuously bother them.

Things really went off the rails when he was thirteen. I thought I was being a nice mom when I sent him to Alaska to visit a friend. He came home smoking. I thought I was being a nice mom when I took him to the park to hang out with some friends. He also met drug dealers there.

I got the call from the police when he shoplifted. I got the call from the school when he slapped a kid on the bus. I *made* the call to the police when he thought he was big enough to push me.

Our son never liked going to school. Even in elementary school, he would say after three or four days that he needed a break. As he got older, it was harder and harder to get him to go. We got the truancy letter from the school district. We had the meetings with his collaboration team about his 504 plan (which allows for classroom accommodations). We drove him to the continuation high school he was assigned to (and then rarely attended).

We constantly struggled with how much he was on the computer. His online friends would help him figure out how to get around any control. We should have just gotten rid of all of the computers, but I felt like my hands were tied – we're a technology focused family in employment, volunteer activities, and relaxation.

Throughout my son's childhood, we tried so many things to help him learn to control his impulses and develop confidence. Martial arts, art therapy, social skills class, Cub Scouts, a therapist that specialized in working with males, behavior modification plans, medication, going to church, and more – we tried them all.

The High School Years

We started looking at residential therapeutic schools and outdoor programs when he was thirteen. It took us an entire extra-long year to pull the plug. It was the hardest decision I have ever made. How do you let go of the image you have of your child, the faith you have in them to turn things around? How do you decide to remove him from everything he's ever known for a year at a minimum? How do you finally admit defeat and send him away?

During this year when we were wavering, I got advice from and vented my anxiety to everyone I could talk to. We met with our minister, who laid it on the line: Did we want this type of prison for our son (residential therapeutic school) or the other type of prison – the real one – for him? It really did look like those were the only two options. It still took us several more months to decide.

But finally the night came when there was a knock on the door at about midnight. Two buff young men came in and we introduced them to our son. We told him that we loved him and he would be going away to a school in Utah. Then we left for about an hour. When we came home, he was gone.

For the first time in years, the lights weren't on all night. There was no one playing video games while watching a movie throughout the night. We knew our credit cards were safe.

He was gone for fifteen months, other than a few visits home. He came home for three months, during which time he went to an alternative private school. Then we had the midnight visit again, and he was back in residential therapeutic for another three months. Back at home, after some changes in the administration of the alternative private school, he convinced us to let him go to a local charter school and I went to bat for him, convincing the principal to give him a chance. Within the first week he was ditching school and hanging out with the wrong crowd. Which is what his friends' parents were saying about him, I'm sure!

At a certain point, we had had enough. Our son's friend offered to let him live with him in Washington, promising to get him to go to school and get a job. We thought, "Fine – you deal with it now." It lasted a week before they were both arrested for breaking and entering because they tore up the house they were living in when the landlord told them they had to leave.

Our son spent three weeks in juvenile hall, and then he got a really amazing break. The thing about our son is, even as he was getting into trouble constantly, there were a lot of people who loved him. He's a personable, intelligent person, and it wasn't just us – his crazy parents – who believed in him. Even when he was in juvenile hall, the guards liked him and gave him extra privileges.

And the prosecutor worked with us. After friends sent letters of recommendation and we submitted a plan of where our son would go when released, the prosecutor offered to let him go and to expunge the record if our son stayed out of trouble with the law for one year.

That's when we sent him to an alternative boarding school in New Hampshire. By this time, he was a senior and all of this effort just to make sure he graduated from high school was looking like it might just pay off.

Until he got kicked out, a month before the end of the school year.

But again, he caught a break. The school let him finish up his school work at home. Finally, that June, we flew to New Hampshire and he graduated with his class. At long last, after many years of struggle and sorrow and tons of money – he had his high school diploma!

Me in All This

So those are the highlights. Some or a lot of what we went through is probably familiar to you. The funny thing is that, at the time, it didn't seem as bad as it sounds now. It just seemed normal, and not because that was just our day to day life.

It's because that's how our relationship had evolved over time, from his earliest days. The relationship was built on my collection of beliefs about parenting and about myself. It generated from those hard-held thoughts that I wasn't enough and I was never heard. It out-pictured how I thought family life was supposed to be based on my views of my own upbringing.

All of these beliefs blocked me from being able to truly help my son, and they certainly didn't make for a happy life for me.

Of course, there were lots of other factors with my son's personality, the way he interpreted events, and his choices on how to react topping the list. Other significant contributors were my husband's childhood issues, my daughter's growing up process, the family dynamic we developed, the school culture, how American society views boys, and the prevalence of online video games.

None of those are actually within my control. What I finally, *finally* realized is that if I wanted a different experience, I needed to start with me.

I realized that it is absolutely, for sure, without a doubt possible to feel and believe differently about myself as a person and as a mom, and that doing so changes everything: how the world responds to me and how I respond to the events in my life. It changes whether I come unglued when my son punches a hole in the wall and let it escalate the overall situation, or if I have the capacity to wait until things have calmed down and I can respond in a way that doesn't widen the division between us.

You'll be reading about many of the limiting beliefs that I had and how I reframed them. Writing this book has brought me even more peace as I worked through additional aspects of those beliefs and recognized how different I am from how I used to be.

What I am especially grateful for is the relationship I have with my son now. I enjoy being around him again! Some of this can be attributed to his own growth and maturation, but I know without a shadow of a doubt it would not have been possible if I had held on to those beliefs and continued to react to my son in the ways I always had. It can, in part, be attributed to my being willing to look within and take action to become the mom and the person that I wanted to become.

CHAPTER 3:

A Simple Tool for Changing Everything

In this book, I'm encouraging you to clear out old beliefs and emotional triggers that aren't serving you. These stuck patterns are making things even harder for you during these teenager years, and you deserve better.

Tapping is a very effective tool for releasing emotional charges and beliefs created through traumatic experiences. This book walks you through the steps for how to do it. You'll:

- Learn how to tap

- Overcome mental blocks or concerns that are stopping you from getting the most out of this process
- Tap on a set of events and beliefs around specific topics that impact your relationship with your teen:
  □ Parenting
  □ Your current situation
  □ Your child
  □ Traits that you think define you
  □ Your deepest beliefs around worthiness
- Finetune your tapping process to correct anything you are doing that reduces tapping's effectiveness

Using the Scripts

In the five chapters on various topics, I provide three to five tapping scripts as examples on how to clear specific feelings and beliefs like guilt, anger, and perfectionism. You will substitute your own events for the ones in the examples, and you can substitute your child's name whenever the scripts say "my son," "my child," or "my teen." You can also use the structure of the scripts to work on feelings or beliefs that aren't covered in this book.

Before each script, I ask you to write down five to ten events that generate the feeling or belief being addressed. You won't need to tap on each one due to what's called the generalization effect. As you clear emotions around specific events, other events for which you have the same feelings will also decrease in intensity. For example, if you tap on a time when you feel guilty because you came unglued on your teen, you will start to feel less guilt around other instances of you losing your temper.

After learning how to tap in Chapter 4, I recommend that you start with Chapter 5 and go through the next chapters sequentially to Chapter 9. Not every issue in these chapters will resonate with you and that's okay; you don't have to tap on them. If you're not sure if one is true for you, here's a trick: close your eyes, tap continuously on your collar bone, and ask yourself, "Was there a time when I felt this way?" Something may or may not come up, and that's okay.

Just reading the lead in to each tapping script may be helpful to you, even before doing the tapping, because you'll see that someone understands your situation. Even if my reasons and interpretations aren't the same as yours, reading them may open you to new understandings of your own motivations, or at least help you feel less alone.

What we're aiming for is that moment of "aha," followed by that shift that signals a release. It's such an empowering moment! I hope you'll love having those moments so much that you get a little addicted to finding issues and releasing them. It can be fun!

How Tapping Works

Before I get into the details of how to tap, I wanted to walk you through how and why it works.

When you were young, you made decisions that certain beliefs are true, based on your knowledge and experience at the time. From then on, everything you've experienced has been run through that belief, like a filter. Your life is currently being run partially by beliefs you made up when you were two, or five, or seven! It's an amazing thought, isn't it?

Many of your beliefs were based on traumatic experiences. Your brain – specifically, the limbic system – stored a memory that it uses to try to keep you safe.

- The hippocampus compares one event to the other and creates connections. For example, if each time you went to pet your grandmother's border collie he would snap at your fingers, you would learn that border collies (or maybe all dogs) are dangerous. Using tapping can break that connection so that the hippocampus knows for future reference that border collies (or dogs) are not scary.

- The amygdala is the source of emotions and long-term memory. It initiates the fight, flight, or freeze response to real or perceived danger. Tapping turns off the amygdala, disrupting the stress response. It allows the brain synapses to be rewired so you have a more appropriate response to a situation that is happening now, not in the past. In other words, the part of you that is still remembering the trauma can now feel safe.

This is how tapping reduces the production of cortisol, increases the production of serotonin, and brings the mind to brainwave frequencies associated with relaxation.

Tapping can also help with physical issues. A study by the Center for Disease Control (CDC) found that those who had the highest amount of emotional trauma as children had higher rates of many diseases as adults, like cancer, heart disease, high blood pressure, obesity, and diabetes. It sure seems to me that it's a good idea to eliminate the emotional connections to childhood traumas!

Tapping may seem far "out there" or too strange for some people. But it is based on Western psychological science, including cognitive therapy and exposure therapy. It is joined with Eastern medicine and the understanding of how pressure on acupuncture points changes the energy system of the body.

There are also many studies that document its effectiveness. EFT is one in a group of therapies called energy psychology. Over 100 research studies, review articles, and meta-analyses on energy psychology have been published in professional, peer reviewed journals. They include randomized control studies and pre-post outcome studies, ninety-eight percent of which document effectiveness of energy psychology methodologies. Go to https://www.energypsych.org/page/Research_Landing for a comprehensive list of studies.

Now that we know some of the science behind tapping, let's learn how to do it.

CHAPTER 4:

How to Tap

In this chapter, you'll learn how to tap, including some tips and tricks to make it as effective as possible and what to do if it doesn't seem to be working. You'll also have a chance to release beliefs you might have about whether tapping will work for you.

But first, I want to cover something important about what makes EFT effective: the concept of aspects.

The Concept of Aspects

To clear the emotional charge from an event, you must tap on all of its aspects, which are the various sensations and feelings you experienced during the event.

An aspect can be a pain, physical sensation, emotion, image, sound, taste, odor, or belief, according to EFTuniverse. com. To thoroughly release an aspect of a memory, it's important to explore what you felt, saw, smelled, tasted, heard, and touched during the event, as well as any beliefs you formed about yourself or the world at the time of the event.

For example, let's say you and your teen are grocery shopping and you start arguing over whether you will take them to their friend's house on the way home. You argue from the moment you get in the car until you arrive home and put away the groceries, then they slam out of the house.

If you tap on "I'm upset" or "I'm angry," you probably won't get the results you want. You'll get more success if you tap on each part of the event that generated an emotional charge in you. It could be when they took for granted that you would take them where they want to go, as if your needs don't matter. It could be the helplessness you felt the moment they slammed the door, effectively stopping communication. You may also have a physical reaction when you remember the slam of the door.

These are all different aspects, and each would need to be tapped on for the emotional charge to be cleared. It's like a table with multiple legs; as you start chopping off legs, the table will topple once enough of the legs have been chopped off.

How to Tap

Now that we've discussed aspects, let's go through how to tap. If this seems overwhelming, don't worry! Go slow until you have the pattern down. You'll get the hang of it pretty quickly, and then you can use it on any stressor in your life. You can also go to www.tappingintoyourtrueself.com/how-to-tap to watch a video on how to tap.

1. Identify an event about which you have an emotional charge (e.g., my son would not stop pestering me about taking him to his friend's house). If a number of events come to mind that all contribute to the emotional charge, pick one that has the highest charge or that calls to you.

2. Write or type everything that you feel or believe about the event (the aspects), being very specific and very honest (e.g., I was so frustrated that he wouldn't stop after I explained why I couldn't, I was really angry that it continued all the way home, I felt helpless when he slammed out of the house).

- Don't be afraid to say your deepest fears or your most embarrassing thoughts or your fiercest anger or hurt. Go for the jugular, as Rob Nelson recommends in his book Hacking Reality.
- The more aspects of the event you identify to tap on, the more success you will have.
- It can be helpful to identify where in your body you feel the most about the event. Do you have a stabbing headache in the right temple, a sharp pain in the pit of your stomach, or a persistent soreness around your heart?

3. Choose one aspect and identify your current distress level about it on a scale of 0 to 10, where 10 is maximum intensity and 0 is no distress (e.g., "the frustration I feel is about an 8"). Take your best guess if you don't know. Write the number down.

4. Repeat a set-up statement one to three times while continuously tapping the Karate Chop point, which is the soft area on the side of the hand (see the large dot on hand diagram below):

"*Even though I feel (or have)* _____
(name the problem),
I deeply love and completely accept myself."

If you feel resistance to saying the end section of the set-up statement ("I deeply love and completely accept myself"), you can still say it anyway or you can say "I accept the way I am feeling right now." This is not trying to force you to think positively. It's about accepting your feelings and beliefs just the way they are. It's important not to sugarcoat them.

5. Then tap two to seven times on each of the additional points in the diagram below, starting at the head, while repeating a brief phrase that reminds you of the problem. For your reminder phrases, use your list of the specific aspects about the event (e.g., "I'm so frustrated," "why wouldn't he stop pestering me," "it's so frustrating that he wouldn't stop").

- Tap using the first two fingers on either your left or right hand on either side of your body. You can also use both hands.
- Tap firmly, but not hard. If you are sensitive, you can tap lightly or in the air over the meridian points while following along in your mind.
- If you are in public, you can still tap! You can unobtrusively rub on the tapping points. If you've found a favorite point that seems to produce shifts for you, just tap on it. Or, believe

it or not, just imagine that you're tapping! I've done this often on public transit.

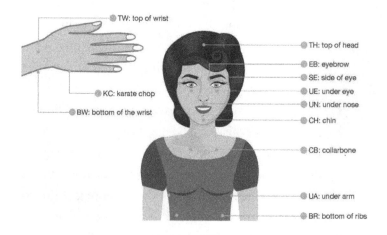

The following abbreviations will be used throughout the book:

KC	Karate chop point
TH	Top of the head
TE	Top of the eye (the inside part of the eyebrow)
SE	Side of the eye
UE	Under the eye (cheekbone)
UN	Under the nose
CH	Under the chin

CB   Collar bone

BR   Bottom of the ribs

UA   Under the arm

TW   Top of the wrist

BW   Bottom of the wrist

6. Stop tapping and determine your distress level again on a scale of 0 to 10. You'll probably feel better already! If there is still a charge, write down your new intensity level (0-10), identify what is contributing to the continued charge, then repeat Steps 4 and 5.

7. If something came up while you were tapping, say a new set-up statement. For example, you may initially be tapping on frustration ("Even though I was so frustrated when…") and after tapping you may feel anger ("Even though I was angry when…").

8. As you feel the intensity of the emotional charge start to decrease, you can add in a reframe. For example, you could say, "I want to get to a calm and peaceful place around this" or "I choose to forgive myself as best I can." The key is to not add in a reframe too soon; be sure to thoroughly tap on the aspects of the event first.

9. Repeat the steps until your distress level gets to 0.

When an item in your list drops to zero, cross it out. If a new aspect comes up, add it to your list and then tap on it.

You may be blown away by memories that come up while you tap. Many times, one will come up that is the core memory that has been driving your emotions and beliefs for many years, and you would never have thought of it as having relevance.

Note: There are times when tapping will bring up a distressing memory. If you become triggered, please take the necessary steps to support yourself. Ideas:

- Drink plenty of water.
- Take a bath with Epsom salts.
- Get plenty of rest.
- Take a walk outside.
- Tap on the memory.
- Call a professional therapist or practitioner.

Tips and Tricks

- When you're writing out your list of the aspects (what you feel and believe) about a certain event, if you get stumped, here's a trick: close your eyes and begin tapping on the collarbone point. Take a deep breath and let it out. Ask yourself, "What do I need to know?" or "What does this mean to me?" while continuing to tap on your collarbone. If nothing comes up, that's fine, but this often helps.

- Test your intensity level often. You can keep tapping on the reminder phrase for as long as you want or until you feel a shift, or you can do shorter tapping rounds. Either way, make sure you test your intensity level after each round.

- If your intensity level goes up after a round of tapping, that's okay! It can be a good thing. It just means that another aspect has risen to the top to be tapped on and released. Look at what came up for you when the level went up, and then tap on it.

- Don't worry about whether you're saying the set-up or reminder phrases the right way. Say them how you feel them. You can literally repeat the same phrase over and over as you tap and it will work. What allows the releasing of emotional charges or limiting beliefs is focusing on the traumatic events, not the words.

- Don't jump to the positive. If you have learned about law of attraction or positive affirmations, you may think you shouldn't dwell on your negative emotions or beliefs, but that's exactly what you need to do for tapping to work. After tapping on the emotions or beliefs, you can add in a reframe, but state what's true and specific to this situation (e.g., "I'm willing to let go of this anger") and not something too generic (e.g., "Everything happens for a reason").

- Tapping doesn't take long – maybe ten to fifteen minutes per event – but if you're having a hard time fitting it in, here's a tip from Rob Nelson's book: try setting a timer for ten minutes. Tap until it dings, then check the intensity level. If there is still an emotional charge, set the timer for another five minutes, then check the intensity level. Keep going until you are at a 0 on the intensity scale.

Basic Process Summary

1. Tune in to how you feel about the event and give it an intensity rating of 0 to 10.
2. State the set-up phrase ("Even though I feel _____, I deeply love and completely accept myself") while tapping on the karate chop point.
3. State reminder phrases as you tap on the other points, starting at the top of the head.
4. Test your feeling intensity level.
5. Repeat until the issue is a 0 on the intensity scale.

Tapping on Resistance

If you're ready to start tapping on issues specific to the situation with your child, feel free to go on to Chapter 5. But if you have any doubt that tapping will work for you, let's tap on that resistance.

Tapping Won't Work for Me

I get that tapping can seem weird at first. It can seem too simple or even too unconventional to be effective (hopefully I eliminated the idea that it's woo-woo in Chapter 3). You also may have tried it before and it didn't work, so you doubt it will this time. Perhaps you've followed along with some of the many EFT videos that are available online; however, many of the presenters are not trained in tapping, and there is some misinformation out there.

You may not want to use tapping because you're already seeing a therapist or other healer and you want to continue it. That's great! Just consider that tapping can complement other modalities. After one tapping session with me, my client Clara's therapist told her that it was the first time she had seemed "Zen" in the years they had been working together.

Or you just may be feeling so overwhelmed, so devastated, so worried about your child that you just can't see how this will help.

Whatever your concern, take a moment to write down everything you think and feel (the aspects) about how tapping won't work for you. Then tap through each one until you feel a shift.

Here's an example (remember to use your words that resonate with you; see the diagram above for the definitions of the abbreviations):

KC	Even though I don't believe tapping will help me with this situation with my teen, I deeply love and completely accept myself.
TH	All this doubt.
TE	How can this possibly help?
SE	I just don't believe it.
UE	It doesn't seem possible
UN	It seems too simple.
CH	Maybe it works for other people, but it won't work for me.
CB	My circumstances are unique and this won't do anything for them.
BR	I just can't see how this will help.
UA	I don't even know why I started looking into this.
TW	It seems ridiculous.

BW	I'm very doubtful.
	After a few rounds, stop and check in. What intensity level are you at now? If it's not 0, what's contributing to the current level? Tap again; start with an updated set-up statement: "Even though I still have some remaining (feelings), I still deeply love and completely accept myself." Continue tapping, checking in every few rounds. As your intensity level drops, you may want to add in some reframes (not too soon!), starting at the top of the head or whatever tapping point you are at. Here is an example of reframing:
TH	I want to trust that this can work.
TE	I want to believe that I can be helped.
SE	Maybe I can let go of my disbelief.
UE	Maybe this is just the thing I need.
UN	If it's helped other people, it can probably help me.
CH	I'll try anything if it will help this situation with my teen – might as well try this.
CB	What have I got to lose?
BR	It may be the best thing that ever happens to me.
UA	Even if it doesn't change things with my child, I'll probably feel better.
TW	I'm willing to try it.

BW	I'm willing to trust that it will help.
	Continue tapping on reframes until you feel complete.

It's My Child's Problem; Why Should I Change?

How I wish I could give you a magic wand to change your child's behavior! This is as close as I can get.

You may have believed me when I said that doing this work isn't about your child; it's for you – for your happiness and peace of mind. But if you have some belief that this situation is your child's problem and that's who should be making some changes, let's tap on that.

Whatever your concern, take a moment to write down everything you think and feel (the aspects) about how it's your child that should make changes. Then tap through each one until you feel a shift.

Here's an example (remember to use your words that resonate with you; see the diagram above for the definitions of the abbreviations):

KC	Even though I don't think this is my problem, and I actually believe it's my child who should be making changes, I deeply love and completely accept myself.
TH	Why should I change?

TE	I'm not causing the problems.
SE	My child is the one getting in trouble all the time.
UE	I'm fine the way I am.
UN	I don't need to make any changes to myself.
CH	That's insulting.
CB	I'm perfectly fine the way I am.
BR	Why isn't the author telling my child to change?
UA	S/he's the one who needs to change.
TW	I'm not the problem – my kid is.
BW	I don't want to change.
	After a few rounds, stop and check in. What intensity level are you at now? If it's not 0, what's contributing to the current level? Tap again; start with an updated set-up statement: "Even though I still have some remaining (feelings), I still deeply love and completely accept myself." Continue tapping, checking in every few rounds. As your intensity level drops, you may want to add in some reframes (not too soon!), starting at the top of the head or whatever tapping point you are at. Here is an example of reframing:
TH	I guess I could try it.
TE	Maybe I'll be happier.

SE	Maybe I'll do it just for myself, to make myself happier.
UE	If it helps with the situation with my child too, I can accept that.
UN	Anything that helps with that is welcome.
CH	I wouldn't mind feeling less stressed.
CB	Maybe it's not about changing me as much as it is about supporting me.
BR	I don't have to change anything I don't want to.
UA	It's entirely up to me; I have the control.
TW	It would feel good to be less stressed.
BW	Why not try it?
	Continue tapping on reframes until you feel complete.

Why Aren't I Good Enough the Way I Am?

You may think that it makes sense for you to work on yourself to change the situation with your child, but if you have some unworthiness beliefs, it may be hard for you to get the most out of this book (more on unworthiness beliefs in Chapter 9).

I struggled for years accepting any advice or input because I took it personally. It seemed like just another someone telling me I wasn't good enough. It definitely held me back from making improvements in my life, from being happier and more peaceful.

So if it seems to you that I'm saying you're not good enough as you are or you're a bad parent or person, it's not true. You are whole and perfect right now, just the way you are.

Whatever your concern, take a moment to write down everything you think and feel (the aspects) about whether this is about you being not good enough. Then tap through each one until you feel a shift.

I want to point out that this tapping script is on a very general topic. I'm including this only so that you can feel some peace toward continuing with the tapping. The actual belief "I'm not good enough" was caused by a number of events in the past, and to release this belief, you need to tap on those specific events and their aspects.

Here's an example (remember to use your words that resonate with you; see the diagram above for the definitions of the abbreviations):

| KC | Even though I'm being told that I'm not good enough just the way I am, I deeply love and completely accept myself. |
| TH | I'm being told I'm not good enough once again. |

TE	I'm always being told I'm not good enough.
SE	Why aren't I good enough the way I am?
UE	I'm a good person.
UN	I'm not as bad as a lot of others.
CH	Now I'm being told that I have to change to help my child.
CB	That seems unfair!
BR	It's not about me; it's about him/her.
UA	But of course, I'm the one that's not good enough.
TW	Why is it always me?
BW	I can't believe this.
	After a few rounds, stop and check in. What intensity level are you at now? If it's not 0, what's contributing to the current level? Tap again; start with an updated set-up statement: "Even though I still have some remaining (feelings), I still deeply love and completely accept myself." Continue tapping, checking in every few rounds. As your intensity level drops, you may want to add in some reframes (not too soon!), starting at the top of the head or whatever tapping point you are at. Here is an example of reframing:
TH	Maybe it's not about whether I'm good enough.

TE	Maybe the author is just trying to support me, to give me new insights.
SE	The author could think I'm fine the way I am.
UE	How would she know if I'm not good enough – she doesn't even know me!
UN	I'll try not to take it personally.
CH	It's not always about me.
CB	I can put aside the concern that I'm not good enough for now.
BR	There will probably be some useful things in this book.
UA	It could end up helping me if I'm willing to try it.
TW	I want to get all of the benefits I can from this book.
BW	I am open to learning all I can.
	Continue tapping on reframes until you feel complete.

Now, on to clearing events and beliefs that could have you stuck parenting in ways that aren't serving you.

CHAPTER 5:

Parent Traps

There's a freaking huge amount of advice on how to parent, isn't there?! And when your teen is behaving badly, there's even more.

We tried them all: behavior modification plans, privilege removals, talking about what was appropriate behavior, etc., etc.

They didn't work.

This is the thing: the way I parented was determined long before my son's behavior escalated and had been active for many years. It was driven by how my own parents parented layered over by my inner wounds and not-so-stellar beliefs about myself. In fact, I think I got the worst of both of my parents – my dad's anger and my mom's victimhood, lack of self-esteem, and deference to authority.

This wasn't going to magically change because I put up a chores chart on the refrigerator.

One of the first steps you can take toward shifting to saneness in your situation is to look at your beliefs about parenting and how they contribute to the issues with your child. Do you parent by being in control or through fear? Do you try to be a friend? Can you not stand to hurt your child's feelings?

It took me a long time to realize that we parented through guilt. We were always trying to guilt our son into behaving properly. When I realized I treated him in a way that I would never treat anyone else, I taught myself to not respond as I always had and start treating him like I would any other person. I had to bite my tongue many times before it became more natural to me, but it really shifted our relationship.

In this chapter, we look at three aspects of parenting: not having faith in your parenting, lack of boundaries, and using control. What other beliefs about parenting do you have that don't serve you?

Lack of Faith in Your Parenting

I was extremely unprepared for parenting. I had never wanted to have children. Then I accidentally and blessedly became a parent.

But I just had no idea how to parent. Truthfully, I believed that children raise themselves. That's what I did, and poorly at that. I had no compass, no road map to tell me what I valued or how to raise children to be self-confident and resilient. I didn't even know it was possible!

It's no wonder I didn't think I could be a good parent. I wanted to be, certainly – I loved my children enough for that. But since I had no sense of myself as a parent, I felt like I had to parent the way others said was the right way. I took advice I didn't feel good about from the school district, doctors, the media, and others – and it pretty much always backfired. I didn't have my children's back sometimes because I went along with other people's advice. Other times I should have taken action about something my children did, but didn't know what, so I didn't do anything.

When we were trying to figure out "what was wrong" with my son in fourth grade, we were referred to a popular local doctor who specialized in ADHD. We paid to have my son go through their diagnostic tools and sure enough, he was diagnosed with ADHD. It didn't really make sense to me based on his behavior, but I thought the doctor must know what he was doing – he was the specialist. My son went on medication, and he promptly began acting *horribly*. He hadn't been mean before but on this medication he was. A different doctor took my son off the medication, but the damage was done; he never quite returned to his former personality.

I also seesawed back and forth between trying to be a disciplinarian and a nurturer. This inconsistency was so confusing for my children! They learned not to trust me, and they learned that I wouldn't always follow through.

I think (I hope!) most parents aren't as clueless as I was. You may be a very conscious parent and now you're finding that your teen's behavior is challenging everything you knew about parenting and yourself. Perhaps you're feeling a little shaky or questioning your parenting choices.

If you have any beliefs that you're not a good enough parent or that others know more about what you should do than you do, you can release them and gain more faith in your ability to know what is best for you and your family.

Impact on Parenting

In my experience, not having faith in your parenting skills:

- Causes you to be inconsistent
- Adds a spark of uncertainty into your parenting, and your smart, rebellious teen will take full advantage of it
- Overrides your inner knowledge that something won't work or is the wrong thing for your child even though the "expert" is recommending it

Sample Script

Write down five to ten beliefs you have about your ability to parent. Write down your feelings about each event. Tap through the events one by one until you feel a shift in how you feel. Here's an example (see Chapter 4 for definitions of the abbreviations):

KC	Even though I didn't agree with the diagnoses and still put my son on ADHD medication, I deeply love and completely accept myself.
TH	I didn't listen to myself.
TE	I was surprised when my son was diagnosed with ADHD.
SE	That didn't seem to be his problem, but I believed the doctor anyway.
UE	I didn't have my son's back.

UN	I let him go on a medication he didn't need and that had negative side effects.
CH	I should have asked more questions and listened to my intuition more.
CB	I should have gotten another opinion.
BR	I wish I hadn't believed that doctor.
UA	I know my child better than any doctor could, and I should have known better.
TW	I harmed my child because I didn't trust myself.
BW	I didn't trust myself.
	After a few rounds, stop and check in. What intensity level are you at now? If it's not 0, what's contributing to the current level? Tap again; start with an updated set-up statement: "Even though I still have some remaining (feelings), I still deeply love and completely accept myself." Continue tapping, checking in every few rounds. As your intensity level drops, you may want to add in some reframes (not too soon!), starting at the top of the head or whatever tapping point you are at. Here is an example of reframing:
TH	I'm not as clueless as I think.
TE	I have good instincts in other areas of my life; I bet I have them here too.
SE	I'm willing to listen to my instincts about parenting.

UE	I know what to do.
UN	I can trust myself to know what to do.
CH	I can know what is the best action for me and my family.
CB	I don't have to take any advice I don't want to follow.
BR	I choose to forgive myself for following that doctor's advice.
UA	I have more parenting skills than I give myself credit for.
TW	I've been a parent all these years – I must have learned something!
BW	I'm willing to trust myself.
	Continue tapping on reframes until you feel complete.

Lack of Boundaries

When my children were young, I lived in a perpetual no-boundary state – especially with my son. And oh my gosh did he develop an entitled attitude! Why wouldn't he, when his mom couldn't say no to him.

I remember this one particular toy from *Dragon Ball Z*. He wanted it and wanted it and wanted it. I finally got it for him. He put it on his shelf and never played with it. He just wanted to have it. This happened fairly regularly.

He knew that if he pestered me enough about something, I would give in, if anything just to make him stop. Great parenting there!

Setting boundaries is a tough one. Many of us are trained as children to please and support others. But you can lose yourself to parenthood if you put everyone's needs in front of your own.

It's not your job to fix others, not even your challenging teen. It's okay to say no. You don't have to anticipate the needs of others or take responsibility for them. You have a right to your own feelings and to express your needs honestly. Boundaries can completely change how you feel about yourself and your world, and can completely change the situation with your teen.

Now if my son wants something from me that I'm not willing to give, I say "no" with the note in my voice that says I mean it, and he accepts it. Maybe he'll ask why not, which is a fair question, but he doesn't question my right to say no.

Impact on Parenting

From my experience, not having good boundaries:

- Creates resentment within you, and it's tough not to strike out at some point when you feel this way

- May mean that you are too permissive, which will likely result in your child struggling academically, exhibiting more behavioral problems than others, and having low self-worth
- Does not teach your children how to set and protect their boundaries so they aren't unduly influenced or taken advantage of by others

Sample Script

Write down five to ten events when you did not have good boundaries. Write down your feelings about each event. Tap through the events one by one until you feel a shift in how you feel. Here's an example (see Chapter 4 for definitions of the abbreviations):

KC	Even though I broke down and bought that toy for my son and once again allowed him to take advantage of me, I deeply love and completely accept myself.
TH	I'm a bit ashamed.
TE	Once again, I did something I said I wouldn't do.
SE	Once again, I didn't hold my boundary.
UE	I suck at having boundaries.
UN	I let my son walk all over me.

CH	It really pisses me off.
CB	I should have the right to say no.
BR	He just takes advantage of me anyway.
UA	I guess it's not his fault that I can't stand firm.
TW	Why do I allow him to walk all over me?
BW	Why do I treat my needs as not important?
	After a few rounds, stop and check in. What intensity level are you at now? If it's not 0, what's contributing to the current level? Tap again; start with an updated set-up statement: "Even though I still have some remaining (feelings), I still deeply love and completely accept myself." Continue tapping, checking in every few rounds. As your intensity level drops, you may want to add in some reframes (not too soon!), starting at the top of the head or whatever tapping point you are at. Here is an example of reframing:
TH	I choose to forgive myself for allowing my son to walk all over me.
TE	I choose to forgive myself for not being able to say no.
SE	I can't really blame my son.
UE	I was the one who didn't know how to set a boundary.
UN	I'm willing to start setting and holding boundaries.

CH	Setting and holding boundaries will make me a better parent.
CB	Setting and holding boundaries is a good way to meet my own needs.
BR	My needs are important and I want to honor them.
UA	I let go of the belief that I have to support and please others.
TW	My son may not like when I set boundaries and that's okay.
BW	I'm going to do it anyway.
	Continue tapping on reframes until you feel complete.

Using Control to Parent

When my son was five, he was upset because he couldn't make any of the family decisions. A friend asked, "Why not let him?" But there was no way I would even consider it. I was in control and had to make the decisions (so they would be the right decisions) and that was all there was to it.

There were early signs that things weren't going well with my children, but I thought if I just kept demanding that everything be done my way, things would work out.

That was a lesson learned too late.

When I think about this, another memory keeps returning to my mind. While we were deep in the difficult situation with my son, I was waiting at a coffee shop while a family with two young boys was placing their order. One of the boys said or did something, and the father raised his hand and feinted that he was going to strike the boy. The father's demeanor was stern and angry in a controlled way. His son jumped away, as if practiced. Later, when they were sitting at a table, the boy scampered around his dad, looking for approval, until the dad finally took him in his lap and hugged him.

How I wanted to have a conversation with that dad. How I wanted to share with him the hard-fought lessons we were learning. How I wanted to let him know that control – even fear – may work in the short term but can cause so many issues later. How I wished I had learned to let up, to allow my children to make their own mistakes, to give guidance and discipline rather than demands.

I sometimes pray for that family, that father and son, and hope that all is well.

Impacts on Parenting

In my experience, using control to parent:

- Backfires eventually because your child learns to feel resentful for not being allowed to have a voice; resentment can drive a lot of seen and unseen disruptive behavior
- Stops you from figuring out your child and their motivations, feelings, and beliefs, which can help you work with your child to change their behavior, and it takes away their freedom to become who they are meant to be
- Can drive a wedge between you, inhibiting the development of a rich, full relationship with your child in which you enjoy them just for being who they are

Sample Script

Write down five to ten events when you used control to parent. Write down your feelings about each event. Tap through the events one by one until you feel a shift in how you feel. Here's an example (see Chapter 4 for definitions of the abbreviations):

KC	Even though I always had to be in control and I didn't allow my son a voice in the family decisions, I deeply love and completely accept myself.
TH	I refused to let my son have a voice.

TE	I wouldn't let him participate in any family decisions.
SE	He was only five; of course he couldn't make the family decisions.
UE	I needed to stay in control and make the decisions.
UN	I was the adult. It was my right to make the decisions.
CH	Besides, I had more information. And I wanted things my way, to make me comfortable.
CB	Whoever heard of allowing a five-year-old to make the decisions?
BR	They're not smart enough to make the decisions. They're just kids.
UA	I wanted to make the decisions and have control.
TW	My son may have started believing his opinions didn't matter, but I didn't want to give up control.
BW	I can't help how he took it; I was dealing with my own needs.

	After a few rounds, stop and check in. What intensity level are you at now? If it's not 0, what's contributing to the current level? Tap again; start with an updated set-up statement: "Even though I still have some remaining (feelings), I still deeply love and completely accept myself."
	Continue tapping, checking in every few rounds. As your intensity level drops, you may want to add in some reframes (not too soon!), starting at the top of the head or whatever tapping point you are at. Here is an example of reframing:
TH	I choose to forgive myself.
TE	At that time I believed I had to stay in control.
SE	I had a belief that if I didn't stay in control, it reflected poorly on me.
UE	I was just trying to get my needs met.
UN	I choose to forgive myself for ignoring my son's needs.
CH	I would choose differently today.
CB	I can't change the past, but I can choose to forgive myself.
BR	I trust my children to make the right decisions for them.
UA	If they make mistakes, I allow them their mistakes and support them in learning from them.

TW	I don't need to be in control all the time.
BW	It's such a relief to let go of some of the control.
	Continue tapping on reframes until you feel complete.

Now, let's look at some beliefs that you have around the current situation with your teen.

CHAPTER 6:

The Dark Days

I bet this is the worst time of your life. It certainly was for me.

When you don't know what your child is going to do next, when you just wish for one moment things would seem normal, when you're scared to pieces that your teen will do something catastrophic, when you have that constant dread in the pit of your stomach – it's pretty awful.

Dealing with the everyday crap is bad enough, but dealing with the fear of the unknown, the uncertainty of whether your child will get through this safely adds that extra spark of horrible.

Then there's that fun feeling like it's your fault. Don't forget the lively duo of shame and embarrassment! And it's just so sad. It was so *not* what you wanted for your child.

You can come to a calmer and more peaceful place around your situation. You can release some of these feelings that are darkening your days. You'll feel better, and you'll be able to think more clearly too. When you eliminate the charge around your emotions about the situation, there's more space for your innate wisdom and cleverness to come through.

In this chapter, we'll start by taking a look at that sense of overwhelm. We'll look at grief, and we'll take on guilt, embarrassment, and shame. Finally, we'll see what we can do to let go of emotions like anger and frustration that are stirred up when the other parent(s) aren't on board. What other feelings do you have about your situation?

Overwhelm

I know how all-consuming this situation can be. It haunts your every moment, hangs over your head like a raincloud. There's a nagging feeling that things are not right with the world. You're constantly thinking about what you can do next to try to get control of this thing. And of course, there's the second guessing, the self-guilting, and the crying to do. Your day is full!

Overwhelm can stop you in your tracks. It just feels so stressful. And the frustration of it can make you want to pull your hair out!

For us, the overwhelm usually came from our son's addiction to online games. Trying to get him to do anything off the computer was a constant struggle. When we put controls on the computer, he would find ways around them. When we took the computer away, he would find someone to give him one.

My husband and I pretty much became hermits. And we went out to dinner a lot. It was a way to get out of the house when the tension and frustration just became too much.

It's okay to take breaks from the worry. It's okay not to worry about your child twenty-four hours a day. It's important to take good care of yourself to relieve the stress and breathe easier. It's just as important as taking steps to help your teen.

Give yourself the same compassion as you would a friend who's going through the same experience.

Impact on Parenting

In my experience, feeling overwhelmed:

- Ignites stress within your body, making you more tired and more prone to becoming ill
- Can make you less effective when searching for solutions – if the stress is bad enough, you won't even try!

- Impacts the rest of your life, which doesn't stop just because your teen has gone off the rails

Sample Script

Write down five to ten events when you felt overwhelmed. Write down your feelings about each event. Tap through the events one by one until you feel a shift in how you feel. Here's an example: (see Chapter 4 for definitions of the abbreviations):

KC	Even though I feel so overwhelmed by my son's addiction to online games, I deeply love and completely accept myself.
TH	I'm so overwhelmed.
TE	This situation is completely consuming me.
SE	I can't hardly think of anything else.
UE	I don't know what to do. How do I get him off the computer?
UN	I feel so overwhelmed by it all.
CH	It's so frustrating not knowing what to do.
CB	This overwhelm is so stressful.
BR	I am really stressed out.
UA	This thing has taken over my life.

TW	It's all I can think about.
BW	I constantly feel like something is wrong.
	After a few rounds, stop and check in. What intensity level are you at now? If it's not 0, what's contributing to the current level? Tap again; start with an updated set-up statement: "Even though I still have some remaining (feelings), I still deeply love and completely accept myself." Continue tapping, checking in every few rounds. As your intensity level drops, you may want to add in some reframes (not too soon!), starting at the top of the head or whatever tapping point you are at. Here is an example of reframing:
TH	I'd like to come to a calm and peaceful place.
TE	I'd like for this stress to lift.
SE	I don't need to hang on to this stress and overwhelm.
UE	Things are going to get done whether I'm stressed and overwhelmed or not.
UN	I can release the need to worry constantly.
CH	Worry and overwhelm don't serve me.
CB	Taking actions to relieve my stress does serve me.
BR	It gives me some separation from this problem.
UA	Everyone deserves a break sometimes.
TW	I deserve a break.

BW	I'm releasing this stress and overwhelm.
	Continue tapping on reframes until you feel complete.

Guilt

I can list for you a litany of things I did wrong when my children were young. I was so angry and yelled a lot. I was controlling and impatient. My emotions were enmeshed with them. I didn't protect them sometimes because I didn't know what to do. I wouldn't stop working on the computer to connect with them. I could go on.

It wasn't actually a surprise to me when my children started having problems as teenagers. I expected it. I believed all teenagers got into trouble, for one thing, but also why wouldn't they have enough emotional issues that they would get into trouble – they had me for a parent!

So yeah, when we were going through such a horrible time with our son, I beat myself up a lot. I knew it was my fault.

I don't actually like the phrase "You did the best you could at the time." To me, it implies that you weren't okay at that time and thank God you're an improved version now. But… I did the best I could at the time. I didn't mean to make my children feel less than or unimportant or (fill in all the other ways I failed them). But I did, because I was grappling with my own self-worth issues and internal drama and big, ugly, sink-hole wounds, and I didn't know diddly-squat about parenting. If I had known differently, I would have chosen differently.

It's true for you, too. You may feel that you deserve to wear a hair shirt the rest of your days for your parenting fails, but it doesn't serve anyone for you to stay stuck in guilt.

Guilt can keep you stuck in grief, fear, and anger, and it magnifies those feelings. Feeling guilty seems like you're doing something (punishing the guilty party) when you're actually keeping things from moving forward. It keeps you in judgement mode – you're judging yourself over and over again for something that is in the past.

You never can know, either, how your child would have turned out if you had done things differently. I'm pretty sure mine wouldn't have been so difficult, but I can't know for sure. He has his own life journey and lessons to learn and his own personality, strengths, foibles, and way of looking at the world. He may have become the exact same teenager he was no matter how I parented.

Impact on Parenting

In my experience, continuing to feel guilty:

- Makes you a martyr and keeps the focus on you, rather than on your child
- Keeps you stuck in a cycle of feeling bad about what was; it would be more beneficial to appreciate today and find solutions for tomorrow.
- Makes it easy to take responsibility and accountability off of your child... maybe there's a little bit of you who prefers taking the blame?

Sample Script

Write down five to ten events that makes you think this situation is your fault. Write down your feelings about each event. Tap through the events one by one until you feel a shift in how you feel. Here's an example (see Chapter 4 for definitions of the abbreviations):

KC	Even though I feel so guilty that I would always keep working on my computer rather than pay attention to my son, I deeply love and completely accept myself.
TH	All this guilt.
TE	I feel really guilty.
SE	I was such a bad mom.
UE	I couldn't even look up from my computer to talk to my son.

UN	I always acted like my work was more important than my son.
CH	Of course he's screwed up!
CB	I taught him that he wasn't important.
BR	I would act out too if that's how my mom treated me.
UA	It's all my fault.
TW	I should have been a better mom.
BW	I'll always feel guilty about this. I deserve to always feel guilty about this.
	After a few rounds, stop and check in. What intensity level are you at now? If it's not 0, what's contributing to the current level? Tap again; start with an updated set-up statement: "Even though I still have some remaining (feelings), I still deeply love and completely accept myself." Continue tapping, checking in every few rounds. As your intensity level drops, you may want to add in some reframes (not too soon!), starting at the top of the head or whatever tapping point you are at. Here is an example of reframing:
TH	I do not want to feel guilty for the rest of my life.
TE	Sure, I made some mistakes. Every parent makes mistakes.

SE	I may feel like my mistakes were worse than most, but they weren't.
UE	I can't keep beating myself up about this.
UN	It doesn't serve me. It keeps me stuck.
CH	I'd like to feel less guilty.
CB	I'm willing to feel less guilty.
BR	I can't change the past, but I can do better in the future.
UA	I release these feelings of guilt.
TW	I allow my son to live his own life free of me feeling guilty.
BW	I choose to forgive myself as best I can.
	Continue tapping on reframes until you feel complete.

Grief

There's such a huge sense of loss when our child chooses a difficult path.

I wanted my son to know how amazing he was. I wanted to go to high school football games and to be the embarrassing mom as I fussed over his prom date. I wanted to be on the Grad Night committee and worry about him not getting his college applications in on time. I wanted what I thought of as a "normal" teenage experience.

My actual experience came nowhere close. It was hard to let go of what I wanted and come to accept the reality. I know that my child has his own path and everything he went through is part of his journey, but I still had to grieve for the lost expectations and the lost opportunities and experiences that I wished for him, and especially knowing that he didn't see himself as I saw him – darling and lovable and sweet and intelligent and funny. That was sad.

You may always feel a little sad about this; you may always wish things had gone differently. And that's okay; it is what it is. But you can acknowledge the loss and give yourself permission to grieve.

Impact on Parenting

In my experience, not acknowledging the loss and grief of this situation:

- Can cause physical issues, such as insomnia
- Can skew toward a victim viewpoint ("why me?")
- Means that you carry the situation with you constantly, like a dark cloud over your heart, insulating you from feeling happy or joyful

Sample Script

Write down five to ten events that cause you to grieve the situation. Write down your feelings about each event. Tap through the events one by one until you feel a shift in how you feel. Here's an example (see Chapter 4 for definitions of the abbreviations):

KC	Even though I feel so sad that my son never went to prom or Grad Night or other rite-of-passage experiences, I deeply love and completely accept myself.
TH	This deep grief.
TE	I feel such a sense of loss.
SE	I am so sad that my son never got to do these things.
UE	I wanted him to experience these things.
UN	He'll never experience them.
CH	It's so sad. I'm so sad.
CB	To me, it's such a loss
BR	I feel so much grief and sadness.
UA	I can't believe he'll never get to do these things.
TW	I wish these things for him.
BW	But they'll never happen.

	After a few rounds, stop and check in. What intensity level are you at now? If it's not 0, what's contributing to the current level? Tap again; start with an updated set-up statement: "Even though I still have some remaining (feelings), I still deeply love and completely accept myself." Continue tapping, checking in every few rounds. As your intensity level drops, you may want to add in some reframes (not too soon!), starting at the top of the head or whatever tapping point you are at. Here is an example of reframing:
TH	I'd like to come to a calm and peaceful place about this.
TE	I acknowledge my sadness.
SE	I accept that I feel sad.
UE	I may always feel a little sad about this.
UN	I accept that I may always feel a little sad about this.
CH	I acknowledge my sense of loss for the expectations and wishes that I had.
CB	But they were just expectations and wishes, and I can let them go.
BR	I choose to be okay that my dreams for my son didn't happen.
UA	I choose to see that there is good in what is happening, too.

TW	I am willing to release this grief.
BW	I am willing to let my heart know peace.
	Continue tapping on reframes until you feel complete.

Embarrassment and Shame

How many times during those years was I asked the dreaded question, "So, how is your son?"

How much do they want to know? Do I tell them that the kids on the bus called CPS on us because we literally tried to carry him to the bus so he would go to school? That he set the divan on the balcony on fire in the middle of the night because he was smoking? That we think he came home higher than a kite the other night? Or that, judging by the number of cars coming by our house, we think he might be selling pot?

Or do I provide an answer that doesn't reveal so much, like "He's okay?"

Sometimes, I was embarrassed to tell people what we were actually going through. Other times, I spewed it forth. I couldn't believe this was my situation, and I couldn't believe my son was acting this way. How had it gotten to this?

I also felt shame because I felt it was a reflection on me. I imagined people wondering how I had produced such a bad kid. It seemed like they could see the mistakes I had made and the maelstrom of emotions I felt, and would shake their head and tsk their tongue judgmentally when I walked away. It was so obvious that I was a lousy parent.

I hated those feelings. I hated that I was in a situation in which I felt them. When they were triggered was probably when I made the biggest mistakes with my son, when I would yell the loudest or say the meanest things or come down on him the hardest. It's when I felt the most separate from him.

If you are embarrassed or feel shame, I wish I could hold your hand, be with you in understanding silence, and give you a hug.

Impact on Parenting

In my experience, continuing to feel embarrassed or shame for the situation:

- Are the hardest feelings to deal with and make you the most miserable
- Will come out at the wrong time and prompt you to act in ways that you've promised yourself you're not going to
- Can affect your sense of self-worth and deservedness in many areas of your life

Sample Script

Write down five to ten events that caused you embarrassment or shame about this situation. Write down your feelings about each event. Tap through the events one by one until you feel a shift in how you feel. Here's an example (see Chapter 4 for definitions of the abbreviations):

KC	Even though I felt so embarrassed and shameful when people asked about my son, I deeply love and completely accept myself.
TH	I have such a sense of shame.
TE	Deep within me, I feel shame.
SE	I must be broken. There must be something wrong with me.
UE	I'm so embarrassed.
UN	Obviously, I'm a terrible parent and a terrible person.
CH	Having to talk about my son brings up such a sense of shame.
CB	I feel terrible.
BR	I'm embarrassed that people will judge me.
UA	They'll know what a terrible person and parent I am.
TW	How else would my son have so many problems?
BW	They'll see all of my failures.

	After a few rounds, stop and check in. What intensity level are you at now? If it's not 0, what's contributing to the current level? Tap again; start with an updated set-up statement: "Even though I still have some remaining (feelings), I still deeply love and completely accept myself." Continue tapping, checking in every few rounds. As your intensity level drops, you may want to add in some reframes (not too soon!), starting at the top of the head or whatever tapping point you are at. Here is an example of reframing:
TH	There are many factors that went into this situation.
TE	I choose to forgive myself, as best I can, for my contributions.
SE	I don't need to feel embarrassed.
UE	I don't need to feel shame.
UN	This situation does not reflect who I am.
CH	This situation does not define who I am.
CB	I am willing to release this shame.
BR	I am willing to release this embarrassment.
UA	I see this situation as a learning journey that does not reflect on my self-worth.
TW	Other people probably don't judge me as harshly as I judge myself.

BW	Most people have been very supportive and I am grateful.
	Continue tapping on reframes until you feel complete.

Other Parent(s) Not on the Same Page

If you're going through this with little to no support from the other parent(s), or worse, outright conflict, my heart truly goes out to you. It makes a bad situation worse.

If you have a blended family, it can get complicated. Maybe the stepfather is supportive but the biological father is not, or vice versa. Maybe you see eye-to-eye with the biological father but not his wife, or vice versa. So many possibilities for conflict!

I did not have this issue – my husband and I were in step with each other – but my friend did. Her newly-moved-in boyfriend gave the ultimatum: your out-of-control daughter or me. Guess who is no longer with his girlfriend?

I'm guessing this lack of cooperation with the other parent(s) brings up anger, resentment, sense of betrayal, frustration, irritation, hurt, and more. There is probably more going on in that relationship than can be covered in this book, but tapping can help take the edge off of the emotional charge. And you never know, when you no longer have that emotional edge, the other person may become more cooperative. Stranger things have happened!

Impact on Parenting

Having an emotional charge regarding the other parent(s) and their lack of cooperation:

- Can prevent you from finding ways or seeing opportunities to gain their cooperation
- Gives your teen an opening to provoke reactions from you to take the attention off themselves
- Adds to your stress and overwhelm when you should be focusing your attention on keeping your teen safe and yourself sane

Sample Script

Write down five to ten events when the other parent was not cooperative or supportive. Write down your feelings about each event. Tap through the events one by one until you feel a shift in how you feel. Here's an example (see Chapter 4 for definitions of the abbreviations):

KC	Even though I'm really angry and frustrated that (other parent's name) does not support me when I try to put limits on our child, I deeply love and completely accept myself.
TH	I'm so pissed!
TE	How dare he contradict me in front of our child?
SE	Doesn't he see how important this is?
UE	I feel so angry and frustrated.
UN	We need to be on the same page.
CH	Our child's life depends on it.
CB	Instead, all he does is push back on me.
BR	He never supports me!
UA	Why doesn't he see what needs to be done?
TW	What a jerk.
BW	I'm so angry with him.

	After a few rounds, stop and check in. What intensity level are you at now? If it's not 0, what's contributing to the current level? Tap again; start with an updated set-up statement: "Even though I still have some remaining (feelings), I still deeply love and completely accept myself." Continue tapping, checking in every few rounds. As your intensity level drops, you may want to add in some reframes (not too soon!), starting at the top of the head or whatever tapping point you are at. Here is an example of reframing:
TH	I want to stop blowing up every time we talk.
TE	This anger is not serving me. It's getting in my way.
SE	I'm willing to let go of this anger and frustration.
UE	I'm willing to see new ways of responding.
UN	I'm willing to forgive myself, as best I can, for getting so angry.
CH	Maybe I can try to see his perspective.
CB	I may still be right, but I can at least see if I can understand where he is coming from.
BR	I'd rather be curious than furious.
UA	Even if we never agree completely, perhaps we can find some common ground.
TW	I can only do this if I release this anger and frustration.

BW	I'm willing to let go of this anger and frustration.
	Continue tapping on reframes until you feel complete.

Next, we 'll look at how you currently feel about your teenager.

CHAPTER 7:

Smells Like Teen Spirit

Your emotions about your teen right now are complicated. They're on a roller coaster of dizzying proportions.

On a good day, when there's some miniscule sliver of improvement showing, you may feel hope, relief, like, love, and even a smidgen of pride.

But then the inevitable drop happens, and you're back to disappointment, anger, dislike, annoyance, frustration, irritation, despair – I could go on, but you know. You've been living them.

Why was it, thirteen or fourteen or so years ago, you thought it was a great idea to get pregnant?

Despite appearances, there is a human being in that teen body, and they are going through *a lot*. There's hormones.

There's life changing before their eyes as they transition from child to pre-teen to teen. There's shifting relationships as kids separate out into their cliques. There's enforced school, which is really only enjoyable for a few. There's the constant comparison-evoking siren of social media, and the purposely-addicting video games. Aren't you glad you aren't them?

How would you treat this person if he or she were not your child? Would you give them more credit and more compassion? Would you take the time to listen or explain more? If you weren't so tied up in the drama, would you like them more?

In this chapter, we'll look at the expectations you may have about your child, if you overly identify with them, and if you just plain dislike them right now. What other feelings do you have about your child?

Expectations

My husband and I are self-motivated. Our parents never had to get on us about going to school or doing our homework. Examples: I was the first person on my mom's side of the family to get a college degree (and then got a master's). My husband was a record-setting swimmer while growing up, swimming four to seven hours a day (he still can get up at 4 a.m. without a problem).

We just assumed our son would be the same.

It took us the longest time to figure out that he is not like us. His motivations are different, his values are different, his way of being is different. We couldn't understand why he didn't just do what he needed to do (like going to school and doing homework) and we assumed that he would eventually shape up and "get it."

This was part of the reason it took us way too long to realize he needed to go into a residential program. It was our own expectations that got in our way.

Sometimes I would think: why can't he be different? Why can't he be more like other kids? Why can't he be easy? Why can't he just do what he's supposed to do? Everybody else does!

It was disappointing that he wasn't what I expected him to be, but it was reality. It was hard for me to give up those expectations.

Perhaps you aren't quite so stubborn. But if you need to let go of expectations of who your child is, it can lead to a sense of relief as you see your child and the situation for what they are, not what you wish them to be.

Impact on Parenting

In my experience, having expectations about who your child is:

- Can prevent you from seeing the reality of the situation, which is necessary to find the next best steps to take
- Sends out signals to your child that he or she is not enough being themselves, which can intensify their anger and outbursts
- Keeps your emotional charge high as you constantly fight against reality

Sample Script

Write down five to ten events when your teen did not meet your expectations of who he or she should be. Write down your feelings about each event. Tap through the events one by one until you feel a shift in how you feel. Here's an example (see Chapter 4 for definitions of the abbreviations):

| KC | Even though I don't understand why my son just doesn't do his homework and feels free to skip school, I deeply love and completely accept myself. |
| TH | Why doesn't he just do it? |

TE	I don't understand.
SE	It's not that hard.
UE	He should just do it.
UN	Everyone else does!
CH	He's so stubborn.
CB	He needs to shape up.
BR	A normal person would just do it.
UA	He needs to be different.
TW	Why does he make it so difficult?
BW	This doesn't make sense to me.
	After a few rounds, stop and check in. What intensity level are you at now? If it's not 0, what's contributing to the current level? Tap again; start with an updated set-up statement: "Even though I still have some remaining (feelings), I still deeply love and completely accept myself." Continue tapping, checking in every few rounds. As your intensity level drops, you may want to add in some reframes (not too soon!), starting at the top of the head or whatever tapping point you are at. Here is an example of reframing:
TH	I'd like to see the situation clearly.
TE	I'd like to see my child for who they truly are.

SE	I may be surprised – the reality may be better than what I thought I wanted.
UE	That would be lovely!
UN	Either way, it would be good to be based in reality.
CH	It will make things easier to deal with.
CB	I will be less stressed when I see things clearly.
BR	I release my expectations of who my child should be.
UA	I forgive myself, as best I can, for thinking my child should be different.
TW	I release the idea that my child should be different.
BW	I accept my child for who they are in all their glory.
	Continue tapping on reframes until you feel complete.

Over-Identification

My son attended a day care program after elementary school, and there was one boy there who just didn't like him. One time, this boy stole a bunch of my son's Pokémon cards out of his locker, and the staff said they couldn't do anything about it. I can't tell you how much this hurt my heart and how much I wanted to get back at that kid.

But truthfully, I don't really know how my son felt about it. I just know I was devastated for him. I was probably more upset than if it had happened to me.

Because I was so sensitive to what could possibly hurt my son, I tried to make things easier on him, to shield him from things that would hurt him. But it was based on my perception of how awful something was, based on what I knew would be hurtful to me, and it was a terrible parenting strategy. My son learned to manipulate my soft heart and became overly self-centered.

Over-identifying creates stress and unhappiness for you – with events that didn't even happen to you! It may seem like they should be important to you, because they happened to *your* child. But you feeling bad doesn't help your child. In fact, it can make things seem worse. Yes, give your child empathy, and then step back and allow them full responsibility and accountability for their lives.

Impact on Parenting

In my experience, over-identifying with your child can:

- Stop you from making the tough decisions that you must make because you don't want to make things hard for them

- Help you stay in denial about your child's real problems and how much help they might actually need
- Take the responsibility off of them to find solutions to problems they are facing – if you feel so bad for them that you take on their problems, they learn that they don't need to change their ways

Sample Script

Write down five to ten events when you felt bad for something that happened to your child. Write down your feelings about each event. Tap through the events one by one until you feel a shift in how you feel. Here's an example (see Chapter 4 for definitions of the abbreviations):

KC	Even though I felt terrible about my son's Pokémon cards getting stolen and I was really upset with the boy who was so mean to him, I deeply love and completely accept myself.
TH	I'm so sad for my son.
TE	What an awful thing to do.
SE	Why did he do that to my son?
UE	I feel so bad for my son.
UN	I'm really angry. It wasn't fair!

CH	What a jerk. He really should have been punished.
CB	He should have had to return the cards and apologize to my son.
BR	I'm so frustrated that nothing was done. Why didn't the staff care more about my son?
UA	Why did this have to happen to *my* son?
TW	It should have never happened.
BW	I don't know if I'll ever get over this anger.
	After a few rounds, stop and check in. What intensity level are you at now? If it's not 0, what's contributing to the current level? Tap again; start with an updated set-up statement: "Even though I still have some remaining (feelings), I still deeply love and completely accept myself." Continue tapping, checking in every few rounds. As your intensity level drops, you may want to add in some reframes (not too soon!), starting at the top of the head or whatever tapping point you are at. Here is an example of reframing:
TH	I want to come to a calm and peaceful place about this.
TE	My feeling angry and sad for my child isn't helping anyone.
SE	It's certainly not serving me.
UE	And it could actually be hurting my child.

UN	It could be stopping me from seeing him as the person he is and providing the help he needs.
CH	It's keeping me stuck.
CB	I am willing to forgive the child who did it.
BR	I am willing to forgive the staff.
UA	I release the belief that I need to feel bad about what happened.
TW	I know that I can support my child more when I let this go.
BW	I'll feel better too!
	Continue tapping on reframes until you feel complete.

Dislike of Your Child

Oh boy, did I not like my son for a while! It was even hard to dredge up a feeling of love for him sometimes. I knew deep down that I loved him, but just couldn't feel it.

There were so many times when I was just so over it. Just done. I couldn't care less – I just didn't want to be around him anymore. I didn't want to keep fighting the uphill battle, to be hated so much, to be dealing with something that so obviously didn't make any sense.

Perhaps it's not a P.C. thing to admit that you don't like your child, but these teens test you beyond your limits. They ignore you unless they need something. They yell and intimidate you to get their way. They are so self-centered that they are clueless, but think they're all that. They steal your credit card to buy someone else's avatar on World of Warcraft (or is that just me?). They are putting themselves, their future, their friends, their family, and their home in danger, and think they have a right to do so.

What's not to like?

Impact on Parenting

In my experience, not liking your child right now:

- Makes perfect sense but can make you feel guilty and worried that it will ever change
- Can push you toward giving up on your child and wiping your hands of the situation if it goes too far
- Will be felt by them, at a time when they need you more than ever, even if they don't think they do

Sample Script

Write down five to ten events when you really disliked your teen. Write down your feelings about each event. Tap through the events one by one until you feel a shift in how you feel. Here's an example (see Chapter 4 for definitions of the abbreviations):

KC	Even though I really didn't like my son since he stole our credit card *again*, I deeply love and completely accept myself.
TH	Oh my gosh, I can't believe he did it again.
TE	I am really not liking him right now!
SE	He used to be one of my favorite people – now I don't even like him!
UE	He is being such a jerk.
UN	I may love him, but I don't like him.
CH	Will he ever be a nice person again?
CB	It's hard to imagine!
BR	I just don't like him right now.
UA	He is *not* my favorite person.
TW	What's it going to take to get him to stop stealing our card?
BW	He's making it so hard to like him.

	After a few rounds, stop and check in. What intensity level are you at now? If it's not 0, what's contributing to the current level? Tap again; start with an updated set-up statement: "Even though I still have some remaining (feelings), I still deeply love and completely accept myself." Continue tapping, checking in every few rounds. As your intensity level drops, you may want to add in some reframes (not too soon!), starting at the top of the head or whatever tapping point you are at. Here is an example of reframing:
TH	I may not like him, but I do love him.
TE	He's going through a tough time right now.
SE	It won't last forever.
UE	He won't be a jerk forever.
UN	He'll grow up someday and be nice to be around again.
CH	I can't imagine it right now, but things will change.
CB	I'm sure there will be a time when I will like him again.
BR	In the meantime, I can hold a higher vision for him.
UA	I can remember who he really is.
TW	I can see him coming through this difficult time with more ease.
BW	I can see him happy again.

	Continue tapping on reframes until you feel complete.

In the next chapter, let's look at some traits that feel like just another part of you but are actually learned behaviors.

CHAPTER 8:

Is That Really You?

When we have a consistent feeling state like anger, we can come to believe that it is just part of who we are – a fixed component of our personality or even our genetic makeup, like brown eyes or curly hair.

Of course, we're born with some personality traits, but I don't think I was born angry, or impatient, or perfectionistic. These "traits" were learned or, perhaps, self-taught as I navigated the powerless period of childhood and the long, difficult process of growing up.

If something is learned, you can learn something new to replace it.

In this chapter, we'll look at some of the feeling states that can become entwined with who you think you are:

anger, impatience, indecisiveness, deference to authority, and perfectionism. What else do you feel has become ingrained within you?

Anger

One of my enduring images of childhood is my dad stomping around the house, his lips pursed in that way he had when he was angry. He had a deep voice that was so loud when he yelled. I think he felt his most powerful when he was angry.

I get why he felt so righteous when he was angry. It can feel so dang good – so empowering! As a child, I didn't feel safe to express my needs, so instead I learned to bottle up my emotions, which led to more and more suppressed anger, and boy can it feel great when it comes exploding out!

Anger was the theme of my early parenting years. I really only felt two emotions at that time: anger and love for my children. I had my heart so walled off with anger that when I started working on releasing it, I felt physical pain.

And, oh, my poor children! They grew up with a really angry mom. I didn't know how to express myself or ask for what I needed, so when I had had enough, it would burst out in an inappropriately loud and angry storm. I won't even tell you about the swear words that would come out, too.

I think about the time I picked up my daughter from first grade to go to the dentist. I asked her what they had done in school that morning, and her insistent reply was, "I don't remember." Well, I remember driving my car down the street yelling at my six-year-old to just tell me what they had done in school that day. She sighed and said, "Fine. We read a book. We went to recess." I'm not sure that bit of information was worth having a screaming fit over.

Apologizing after an angry outburst is always called for and models appropriate behavior for your child. For me, though, it doesn't take away the sting of guilt and regret, and I'd much rather be consistently calm because I haven't allowed my anger to build up.

Anger may feel empowering; it may get you what you want in the short term. It can be a helpful indicator that something is out of alignment. But over the long term, too much of it is toxic for your relationship with your child.

Impact on Parenting

In my experience, feeling and acting out of anger:

- Leads you to say or do things you will regret later and that your child, who never forgets, can turn against you

- Gives your teen permission to lash out when they are angry, unless you think it's okay for you and not for them, in which case your teen will (rightly so) call out your hypocrisy
- Can alert you when something is stepping over your boundaries, and then it's important to pay attention to the message while also being aware of how you express the anger

Sample Script

Write down five to ten events when your anger with your child was over the top. Write down your feelings about each event. Tap through the events one by one until you feel a shift in how you feel. Here's an example (see Chapter 4 for definitions of the abbreviations):

KC	Even though I screamed at my daughter because she wouldn't tell me what I wanted to know, I deeply love and completely accept myself.
TH	I was so angry!
TE	And really frustrated and irritated.
SE	What's so hard about telling me what I want to know?
UE	I have a right to my anger.

UN	I can be angry if I want to be.
CH	Anger gives me power.
CB	Anger gets me what I want.
BR	I'm the adult and she should have listened. Of course I was angry!
UA	Who wouldn't be angry?
TW	My anger surges through my body and out my mouth.
BW	My anger can be hard to control.
	After a few rounds, stop and check in. What intensity level are you at now? If it's not 0, what's contributing to the current level? Tap again; start with an updated set-up statement: "Even though I still have some remaining (feelings), I still deeply love and completely accept myself." Continue tapping, checking in every few rounds. As your intensity level drops, you may want to add in some reframes (not too soon!), starting at the top of the head or whatever tapping point you are at. Here is an example of reframing:
TH	Anger may feel empowering, but it doesn't serve me most of the time.
TE	I say things I later regret.
SE	I say hurtful things I don't mean.

UE	I choose to forgive myself, as best I can, for responding out of anger.
UN	I don't deny my anger; it has its purpose.
CH	I can use my anger when it is appropriate to protect myself or my loved ones.
CB	I can use my anger as a sign post that there's something to be aware of.
BR	I also choose not to respond or react in anger as best I can.
UA	My anger does not define me.
TW	I trust myself to find ways to respond kindly even when I'm angry.
BW	I am not an angry person.
	Continue tapping on reframes until you feel complete.

Impatience

Impatience went hand-in-hand with anger as my main parenting tool. Even when I would tell myself to be patient, it wouldn't take me long to flip out.

Here's an example of my impatience: one day, my young daughter and I were going to the store. In the parking lot, I stopped behind a car with its backup lights on. When the driver didn't immediately pull out of the parking space, I waved my hand emphatically to tell her to get the heck out of the space. As she drove away, she yelled out her window, "Have some patience!" My response was, "Shut up!"

I always felt so much pressure to do more, be more, get to the next place. I felt self-generated judgment that other people would think I wasn't good enough if I didn't get something done right away.

And children – well, you know how children can dawdle. What a recipe for disaster, with their very normal behavior and my insane levels of impatience.

Remember how I said I didn't know how to express what I needed in the Anger section? It actually was more than that. I believed my needs were not important. By believing everyone else's needs were more important than my own, I set myself up for outbursts of impatience because I always felt they were never going to be met.

If you also believe that your needs are less important than those of the other people in your life and it presents as impatience, I see you, I acknowledge your needs, and I validate that you are important.

Impact on Parenting

In my experience, being impatient as your default:

- Has you plow right through your children's very human needs of being heard and seen
- Isn't a character trait that you're stuck with – as you learn to take care of yourself, validating your needs as important, you will be less impatient
- Makes it tough to just let something be and let it get worked out naturally and easily

Sample Script

Write down five to ten events when you were outstandingly impatient. Write down your feelings about each event. Tap through the events one by one until you feel a shift in how you feel. Here's an example (see Chapter 4 for definitions of the abbreviations):

KC	Even though I was so impatient because that lady didn't pull out of the parking space fast enough for me, I deeply love and completely accept myself.
TH	I felt so much impatience.
TE	Why didn't she get the heck out of the way?
SE	Get out of the way, lady!
UE	Can't she see I'm in a hurry?
UN	Doesn't she care I'm in a hurry?
CH	I can't stand this waiting.

CB	I need this to happen right now.
BR	Isn't my need important?
UA	Why are my needs never met?
TW	Why are other people's needs more important than my own?
BW	It makes me feel so impatient.
	After a few rounds, stop and check in. What intensity level are you at now? If it's not 0, what's contributing to the current level? Tap again; start with an updated set-up statement: "Even though I still have some remaining (feelings), I still deeply love and completely accept myself." Continue tapping, checking in every few rounds. As your intensity level drops, you may want to add in some reframes (not too soon!), starting at the top of the head or whatever tapping point you are at. Here is an example of reframing:
TH	My impatience doesn't serve me.
TE	Sometimes it even embarrasses me.
SE	I choose to feel less impatient.
UE	I forgive myself, as best I can, for being so impatient.
UN	The driver was just getting ready to back out, not purposely trying to thwart me.
CH	Other people's needs aren't more important than my own.

CB	My needs are important too.
BR	I choose to forgive myself, as best I can, for believing that other people's needs are more important than my own.
UA	I choose to be gentler with myself.
TW	I choose to believe that having needs does not make me a bad person.
BW	I am worthy of having my needs met.
	Continue tapping on reframes until you feel complete.

Indecisiveness

Did you know that I'm indecisive because I'm a Libra? Yep, God's honest truth. It's just the way I was born.

It couldn't be because of all the times growing up that I was told that I was wrong and the beliefs I formed around this happening. Like that time when mom threatened us kids with a spanking if we walked on her clean floor right after she mopped and so, when I really, really had to go to the bathroom, I decided to go in the side yard so I wouldn't get in trouble. Then I got in trouble. I think I even got a spanking.

I had made the wrong decision *again*.

Over time, I learned it was better not to make a decision, to keep my mouth shut and wait it out until someone else makes the decision, or even to ask, "What do you think?" (This is followed by a feeling of, "Whew! Dodged that bullet!")

If there ever is a time to have more confidence in your ability to make decisions, it's when your teenager is being challenging. Not being able to make a decision can mean you have to live with the situation that much longer.

As I've mentioned earlier, it took us a year to decide to send our son to residential therapeutic school, and that was a year when he could have been healing and learning how to handle his feelings rather than cementing the troubling behavior.

By being indecisive, you are actually making a decision. You are deciding not to take action. If this is what you are going to do, then own it. Make it a conscious decision and then set a deadline to revisit the choice. For example, consciously decide not to send your child to residential therapeutic school at this time and revisit it in three months.

Impact on Parenting

In my experience, feeling indecisive:

- Often means a decision is not made and the "default" path is taken; this leaves it pretty much in your child's hands and not yours
- Can provide more time for your teen to take an action that impacts the rest of his or her life
- Drains your self-confidence and generates more indecisiveness

Sample Script

Write down five to ten events from your childhood when you were punished or shamed for a decision you made. Write down your feelings about each event. Tap through the events one by one until you feel a shift in how you feel. Here's an example (see Chapter 4 for definitions of the abbreviations):

KC	Even though I got in trouble when I went to the bathroom in the yard and I felt bad for making that decision, I deeply love and completely accept myself.
TH	I made the wrong decision.
TE	I made the wrong decision again.
SE	I never decide right.
UE	I think I'm making the right decision and then it's wrong.

UN	How was I supposed to know I could go to the bathroom?
CH	I was trying to be a good girl and listen to my mom.
CB	Instead I got in trouble.
BR	I always get in trouble when I make a decision.
UA	Making decisions is hard.
TW	I never have all of the information I need to make a decision.
BW	I hate making decisions.
	After a few rounds, stop and check in. What intensity level are you at now? If it's not 0, what's contributing to the current level? Tap again; start with an updated set-up statement: "Even though I still have some remaining (feelings), I still deeply love and completely accept myself." Continue tapping, checking in every few rounds. As your intensity level drops, you may want to add in some reframes (not too soon!), starting at the top of the head or whatever tapping point you are at. Here is an example of reframing:
TH	It was unfair that I got in trouble.
TE	I was only five and made the best decision I could.
SE	I shouldn't have gotten in trouble.
UE	My mom didn't know she was hurting my ability to make decisions.

UN	She was trying to teach me something.
CH	I took it to mean that I was terrible at making decisions.
CB	I release this belief.
BR	I choose to forgive my mom.
UA	I choose to forgive myself, as best I can, for thinking I made the wrong decision.
TW	I trust in my ability to make decisions.
BW	I make good decisions easily.
	Continue tapping on reframes until you feel complete.

Deference to Authority

I was trained from an early age to defer to authority. My mom also grew up deferring to authority and she passed it on. Having grown up poor out in the country with little understanding of the ways of the world, I think she thought everyone had more power than her.

During those years when our son was beyond misbehaving, we trusted in the school system. We thought that since they dealt with kids all the time, they must know what they were doing. We also didn't feel like we had the choice to push back or demand something different. Plus, I think we were so overwhelmed and gobsmacked that we were willing to let someone else be in charge. I, in particular, kept hoping someone else knew how to fix the problem.

We also trusted the medical field, although it was clear that the way the system worked wasn't in our best interest. Fifteen minutes with a psychiatrist to evaluate the need for medication was, and is, a joke. To devote that little time for something that is so impactful on a person's health is not sufficient.

I feel let down by both the school and the medical system, and yet I can only blame myself. I forgot that both systems are filled with humans who, like all humans, make mistakes or have bad judgment or are new and not yet experienced. The school and the medical establishment also have different motivations than we did as parents.

I gave my power to them.

For example, our son was going to a high school specifically for kids with behavioral issues. At one point, the administration put him on home schooling and then kept him there almost four months, which is against their policies, and they did not follow the required procedures for setting it up. We only found this out by talking to another parent. Instead of making waves, I accepted that this was just the way it had to be.

I wish I had trusted myself more and the authorities less.

Impact on Parenting

In my experience, deferring to authority figures:

- Takes the power out of your hands
- Gives you permission not to make decisions or take the actions that you should take
- Can make you question your own wisdom and override your knowledge of your child and the details of the situation – you're the one living it every day, not them

Sample Script

Write down five to ten events when you deferred to an authority figure against your better judgment. Write down your feelings about each event. Tap through the events one by one until you feel a shift in how you feel. Here's an example (see Chapter 4 for definitions of the abbreviations):

KC	Even though I should have questioned when my son was put on home study, I deeply love and completely accept myself.
TH	I accepted the school district's decision.
TE	I should have questioned it.
SE	I didn't feel I had the right.

UE	I thought they knew what they were doing.
UN	I thought they would know the right thing to do.
CH	I should have known better.
CB	I shouldn't have been so gullible.
BR	I should have asked more questions and done more research.
UA	But I always give in to authority figures.
TW	That's what I'm supposed to do.
BW	I give them power over me.
	After a few rounds, stop and check in. What intensity level are you at now? If it's not 0, what's contributing to the current level? Tap again; start with an updated set-up statement: "Even though I still have some remaining (feelings), I still deeply love and completely accept myself." Continue tapping, checking in every few rounds. As your intensity level drops, you may want to add in some reframes (not too soon!), starting at the top of the head or whatever tapping point you are at. Here is an example of reframing:
TH	I want to take my power back.
TE	I want to be in control over my decisions and my life.
SE	No authority figure knows it all.

UE	I know better what's right for me and my child than the school district does.
UN	I have a right to stand up for myself and my child.
CH	I don't have to be a jerk about it, but I can stand up for what I need.
CB	I wonder if they would be grateful if I took more control.
BR	Or we could be really good partners, with me as the lead.
UA	It's my child, so I have more at stake.
TW	My child is just one kid to them, but he's everything to me.
BW	I have the right to ask for what I want and need.
	Continue tapping on reframes until you feel complete.

Perfectionism

Me, a perfectionist? Whatever gave you that silly idea?

Sure, I would take homework assignments out of my children's hands and finish them, but they had to be done right. And yeah, I freak out when the toilet seat lid is left up, but that's normal, right? And my family knows to go into full court press to clean the house if anyone is coming over, but everyone does that! And…Okay, I see your point.

The thing about perfectionism is that it sounds like it's about being perfect. It's not. It's about the opposite: the fear of failure or of being judged as less than.

The need to be perfect can fuel anxiety and depression. It means that you only like something – or someone or yourself – when it reaches a certain level of perfection, as judged by you. It sets you up for comparing yourself to others (and why being on social media all the time is demoralizing when you are already a perfectionist).

Perfectionism can also lead to procrastination. After all, if you can't do something perfectly, don't even try!

It's time to give yourself a break from the impossibly high standard of perfection.

Impact on Parenting

In my experience, perfectionism:

- Is a very effective way to make your child believe that they are less than, not good enough, or insignificant; they turn around and express this through rebellion, anger, self-harm, or other ways
- Means you can never let your guard down because you're always striving for perfection, so you have a

harder time just enjoying being in the moment with your child

• Teaches your children that it's not okay to make mistakes

Sample Script

Write down five to ten events when your perfectionism took over and caused you stress. Write down your feelings about each event. Tap through the events one by one until you feel a shift in how you feel. Here's an example (see Chapter 4 for definitions of the abbreviations):

KC	Even though I would finish my child's homework so that it was done right, I deeply love and completely accept myself.
TH	I feel this drive to be perfect.
TE	I can't stand the idea of the homework not being done perfectly.
SE	It irked me that it wasn't being done correctly.
UE	So I took over and got it done right.
UN	I like when things are done as close to perfect as possible.
CH	It really bothers me if things aren't done correctly.

CB	I beat myself up when I don't do or say something perfectly.
BR	Everyone strives to be perfect.
UA	Wanting something to be perfect is normal.
TW	I often won't start something unless I know I can do it perfectly.
BW	I know I should relax, but I'm just trying to make everything perfect.
	After a few rounds, stop and check in. What intensity level are you at now? If it's not 0, what's contributing to the current level? Tap again; start with an updated set-up statement: "Even though I still have some remaining (feelings), I still deeply love and completely accept myself." Continue tapping, checking in every few rounds. As your intensity level drops, you may want to add in some reframes (not too soon!), starting at the top of the head or whatever tapping point you are at. Here is an example of reframing:
TH	This perfectionism is driving me crazy.
TE	It keeps me focused on impossible standards.
SE	I would like to release the need to be perfect.
UE	I never can be perfect, so letting go of it as an ideal relieves me.

UN	It's so much less stressful when I don't feel the need to be perfect.
CH	Not aiming for perfect doesn't mean I don't have high standards.
CB	I would just have more realistic standards.
BR	Things can still be done really well even when they're not perfect.
UA	I can be better than perfect – I can enjoy life!
TW	I choose to forgive myself, as best I can, for holding myself to such unattainable standards.
BW	There are things in life more important than being perfect, and I choose to experience them.
	Continue tapping on reframes until you feel complete.

Finally, let's look at some of the deeper negative beliefs you may have about yourself.

CHAPTER 9:

Your Deepest Beliefs

Every single one of us comes out of childhood with negative beliefs about ourselves. When you see events through a child's understanding, you misinterpret them and almost always decide they reflect on who you are or that the world is scary. That's just how a child's mind works.

Some events and your interpretation of them impact you more than others. My top picks:

- Those that make you believe you are unworthy
- Those that leave you carrying shame
- Those that create the belief that you are not safe

Some of the events that create these beliefs may seem small, too minor to have had such a huge impact on your life. But as an EFT practitioner, I find that some of the biggest, hairiest, most limiting beliefs stem from seemingly insignificant, everyday events. My own experience demonstrates this: an event that for years could have me instantly in tears was when my mom criticized how much dirt I had gathered sweeping my grandmother's kitchen.

Other events that create these beliefs are traumas with a capital T. If you have experienced a Big T trauma, such as assault, war, major accident, or abuse, I urge you to work with a certified EFT practitioner, licensed therapist, or other professional to help you. If you are currently seeing a therapist or other professional, EFT can be helpful used in conjunction.

For our purposes, these worthiness, shame, and fear beliefs can play a major role in how you parent. They color how you see your child and the events currently taking place. For example, if you believe you are insignificant, you will interpret your child's behavior as another sign that you are insignificant, when in actuality the behavior has nothing to do with you. If you have a belief that the world is not safe, you may overreact to a fairly harmless event, such as a minor car accident.

These types of beliefs can have many, many aspects. It may take extra persistence to release them. I say go for it!

Working through these core issues can have a tremendous benefit to your life. Letting these suffocating beliefs go can change everything for you!

Unworthiness

Unworthiness has many different flavors. Which of the following resonates with you?

-	I'm unlovable	-	I don't belong
-	I'm not wanted	-	I'm bad
-	I don't believe in myself	-	I'm unworthy
-	I'm broken	-	I'm not important
-	I'm worthless	-	I can't grow up
-	I'm powerless	-	I don't matter
-	I'm invisible	-	It's someone else's fault
-	I'm helpless	-	I don't measure up
-	I'm inadequate	-	I'm not capable
-	I'm stupid	-	I never get it right

There's not many in that list that I haven't thought or said about myself at one point or another, but probably my top two are "I'm so stupid" and "What an idiot." They're my own special way of beating myself up after embarrassing myself or making a mistake.

A classic story in my house is the Christmas that we got my son his first bike. I was cleaning up when my husband came into the room and said that our son had done great riding the bike. I completely lost it. I cried all afternoon. I didn't get to see my son ride his bike for the first time and this obviously meant that I was insignificant and my needs didn't matter. I was a terrible mom. How could I think that I could ever be the happy mom proudly watching her son riding his bike? Etc. All afternoon.

But when you have a deep sense of unworthiness, even the innocuous things can trigger a firestorm of self-flagellation.

Impact on Parenting

In my experience, feeling unworthy:

- Can lead to depression, zapping the energy you need to take action
- Can prevent you from accessing your highest wisdom; if you don't believe in yourself to be worthy or capable of transforming the situation, you can be blocked
- Can paralyze you; if you don't believe you are worthy of success or you aren't important enough for the right help to come your way, why try?

Your Deepest Beliefs | 121

Sample Script

Write down five to ten events when you felt unworthy. Write down your feelings about each event. Tap through the events one by one until you feel a shift in how you feel. Here's an example (see Chapter 4 for definitions of the abbreviations):

KC	Even though I was hurt and upset about not seeing my son ride his bike for the first time because I saw it as a reflection of my insignificance, I deeply love and completely accept myself.
TH	I feel so insignificant.
TE	My husband couldn't even wait for me to be there to watch my son.
SE	It wasn't important that I was there.
UE	I'm obviously not important.
UN	I was excited to see my son ride his bike for the first time but I didn't get to.
CH	It's not important for me to get what I want.
CB	Because I'm insignificant.
BR	I was stupid to think that I would get to see my son ride his bike for the first time.
UA	I can't believe I missed out on that milestone.
TW	I'll never be able to make it up.

BW	I'm so stupid.
	After a few rounds, stop and check in. What intensity level are you at now? If it's not 0, what's contributing to the current level? Tap again; start with an updated set-up statement: "Even though I still have some remaining (feelings), I still deeply love and completely accept myself." Continue tapping, checking in every few rounds. As your intensity level drops, you may want to add in some reframes (not too soon!), starting at the top of the head or whatever tapping point you are at. Here is an example of reframing:
TH	This was just a misunderstanding.
TE	My husband didn't know I wanted to be there.
SE	It's not a reflection on who I am or my worth.
UE	My husband was just excited about getting my son on the bike.
UN	He had no clue it was important to me.
CH	I choose to release these feelings of insignificance.
CB	I can see this event for what it was, a misunderstanding.
BR	It wasn't about me and how worthy or unworthy I am.
UA	I know that if my husband knew it was important to me, he would have made sure I was there.

TW	He always believes in me.
BW	I can believe in myself.
	Continue tapping on reframes until you feel complete.

Shame

Shame is different from embarrassment. Embarrassment comes from feeling bad about something you did. Shame comes from feeling bad about who you are.

Events that generate shame can be the hardest to talk about. No one wants to bare the moments of their greatest shame. And yet bringing those events to the light of day is the only way to release the shame. Just saying them out loud takes away some of their power. Just saying them out loud helps you see them for what they are: events that happened in your life that have nothing to do with your worth as a person.

For years, I felt so much shame for a time I hit my cousin. My aunt had taken me with my cousins to stay at the beach. We were out to dinner and my youngest cousin, the only boy in the family, hit his sister, the cousin I was closest to. She complained to her mom, who did nothing, and since I felt it was unfair, I hit him one time on his arm. He deserved it, I thought. You would have thought I had committed an egregious sin. My aunt dressed me down, and that was the last time I was invited to go to the beach. For years, this episode made me feel like such a bad person.

Shame is such a debilitating feeling that worms its way into every corner of your heart. But I'm here to tell you: you did not and do not deserve to feel shame. You are perfect and whole just the way you are.

Impact on Parenting

In my experience, feeling shame:

- Can trigger you to react in incomprehensible ways; because the shame stays hidden, your actions can make no sense to your family
- Can create barriers for you to connect with others at a deeper level
- Puts limits on how much happiness or joy you have in your life

Sample Script

Write down five to ten events when you felt shame. Write down your feelings about each event. Tap through the events one by one until you feel a shift in how you feel. Here's an example (see Chapter 4 for definitions of the abbreviations):

KC	Even though I was so ashamed when I hit my cousin and got in trouble for it, I deeply love and completely accept myself.
TH	I feel so much shame.
TE	I shouldn't have been bad.
SE	I should be a better person.
UE	I don't know how to act properly.
UN	My instincts are wrong.
CH	I shouldn't have hit my cousin; that was bad.
CB	I'm so ashamed.
BR	I guess I was raised wrong, if I would hit my cousin.
UA	Or maybe I'm just a bad person.
TW	Otherwise I would know not to hit someone.
BW	I feel shame for what I did.

	After a few rounds, stop and check in. What intensity level are you at now? If it's not 0, what's contributing to the current level? Tap again; start with an updated set-up statement: "Even though I still have some remaining (feelings), I still deeply love and completely accept myself." Continue tapping, checking in every few rounds. As your intensity level drops, you may want to add in some reframes (not too soon!), starting at the top of the head or whatever tapping point you are at. Here is an example of reframing:
TH	In the scheme of things, what I did wasn't that bad.
TE	I thought it was only fair.
SE	I was trying to make things right, and just made a mistake.
UE	I did it out of love for my cousin.
UN	It doesn't make me a bad person.
CH	I took my aunt's admonishment too personally.
CB	I can still believe I did the right thing, even if my aunt didn't.
BR	My instincts may have been fine; my aunt just saw things differently.
UA	I'm not a bad person.
TW	I choose to forgive myself, as best I can, for feeling shame about this incident.

BW	Making a mistake does not mean that I should feel shame.
	Continue tapping on reframes until you feel complete.

Fear

One time I left my sweater on the playground at school. I think I was about seven. I still vividly recall the spanking I got – my dad holding me by the hand and spanking me with the other as I ran in circles trying to get away.

That event stays with me not just because I wasn't safe physically. I also felt unsafe emotionally. I was powerless to protect myself. I learned it's not safe to make a mistake, that judgment will be swift and harsh. How much time of my adult life have I tried to make myself feel safe by trying really hard not to make any mistakes?

There are so many things that can make us decide that we are not safe and/or the world is not safe. The anxiety of constantly feeling unsafe is not only detrimental to your health; it limits how you experience life and how much joy you feel.

Impact on Parenting

In my experience, feeling unsafe:

- Can make you be overly conservative and not take chances, which limits your choices
- Can cause you to overly protect your children, not giving them the chance to stretch and grow
- Will have you avoid new experiences and harshly judge others

Sample Script

Write down five to ten events when you felt fearful. Write down your feelings about each event. Tap through the events one by one until you feel a shift in how you feel. Here's an example (see Chapter 4 for definitions of the abbreviations):

KC	Even though I was so scared when my dad was spanking me, I deeply love and completely accept myself.
TH	I was so scared!
TE	I tried my best to get away, to protect myself.
SE	But I was too little.
UE	I was powerless to protect myself.
UN	It was so scary!
CH	I was only five and this was a very normal way to react.

CB	My dad was so much stronger and bigger than me, and he was so angry.
BR	My dad thought he was doing the right thing.
UA	But it scared me to pieces.
TW	I learned that it's scary to make mistakes.
BW	I learned I will be punished if I make mistakes.
	After a few rounds, stop and check in. What intensity level are you at now? If it's not 0, what's contributing to the current level? Tap again; start with an updated set-up statement: "Even though I still have some remaining (feelings), I still deeply love and completely accept myself." Continue tapping, checking in every few rounds. As your intensity level drops, you may want to add in some reframes (not too soon!), starting at the top of the head or whatever tapping point you are at. Here is an example of reframing:
TH	I'm not little anymore.
TE	I can protect myself now.
SE	I no longer have to be afraid of being spanked.
UE	I now know that making mistakes is very normal.
UN	It's how we learn.
CH	I'd like to come to a calm and peaceful place about this.

CB	I choose to forgive my dad for scaring me.
BR	I release the fear that I've held on to for all of these years.
UA	I can leave my sweater anywhere, and it's no big deal.
TW	I am safe.
BW	I choose to feel safe no matter where I go or what I do.
	Continue tapping on reframes until you feel complete.

If you're still not sure that you're doing tapping right or you think you should be getting more from it, in the next chapter we'll look at ways you may be hampering tapping's benefits.

CHAPTER 10:

Will This Actually Work?

If you bought this book but still aren't sure tapping is for you, let me ask: what are you willing to do for your child? I'm guessing your answer is anything – and this is the anything.

I'm convinced things started to turn around with my son when I became aware of how I was parenting and changed it. This is not to take away the amazing work and changes my son made – I'm very proud of him. But it absolutely was a key part of it.

Take the chance. If you feel resistance to tapping, revisit the scripts in Chapter 4 or, if those are not the reasons for your resistance, tap on your reasons. If you need someone to make you accountable, find a certified practitioner to work with (almost all of them will work with you online or by phone).

If you've been tapping on an issue and have not been feeling a shift, it's probably because of one or more of the following.

- You missed an aspect (see Chapter 4 for the definition of an aspect). Review the event and look for any additional aspects (things you saw, heard, smelled, tasted, touched or felt) and tap on them.
- You aren't being specific enough. Tapping on something general (e.g., "I am upset") won't work. The more specific the event (e.g., "I'm so upset that my teen ditched school for the third time in two weeks and lied about it again"), the more likely you will get to the core issue and all of its different aspects.
- You didn't tap long enough on the event, or you added in reframes too early. Try again, this time tapping on the negative emotions and beliefs at least ten to fifteen minutes.
- The issues addressed in this book don't resonate with you, or there are others that are bigger for you. You can use the process you've learned here to tap on the issues that do resonate with you.

- You have what's called a secondary gain. This means you get some benefit from keeping your problem. For example, if you know your anger is easily triggered and it's causing issues in your relationships, you may not want to let it go because it gives you a sense of safety or power. You can tap on your secondary gain.

- If it seemed like tapping was working and then it stopped, or if you know you should change something but you can't find the energy to do it or you self-sabotage, you may have your wires crossed (it's called a psycho-energetic reversal). You'll actually be attracted to the opposite of the good outcome that you want.

Psycho-energetic reversals tend to happen because you believe it's not possible, it's not safe, or you don't deserve to let go of an issue, because you won't know who you will be without it, or because you're just not willing to let it go, according to the Association for Comprehensive Energy Psychology.

The set-up statement while tapping on the karate chop point often will shift a psycho-energetic reversal. If this doesn't work, tap on all potential causes of the reversal.

Here's a set-up statement you can adapt:

"Even though I have this problem, and even if I don't deserve to get over this problem, and even if it's not possible for me to get over this problem, I deeply love and completely accept myself. Even if it's not safe for me to get over this problem and even if I'm not willing to get over this problem, I deeply love and completely accept myself. Even if I would not know who I am if I get over this problem, I deeply love and completely accept myself."

- There is an underlying medical issue. Tapping does not replace medical care. Make sure you see your doctor for physical or psychological conditions before you begin using tapping.

- There are other events that are causing the belief or traumatic memories. You may be subconsciously blocking memories from coming up. A therapist or practitioner may be able to help you identify and then safely work through the hidden event.

- While you can get great results doing tapping on your own, it can be difficult sometimes. It can be hard to see your own situation clearly. In this case, you may want to work with a certified practitioner, who can help you see patterns and beliefs that you can't see by yourself. Another benefit of working with a practitioner is the power of being seen and heard by someone outside of your situation.

Finally, you have to be willing to own your internal drama. You have to be willing to admit to yourself the beliefs that you hold and how you've messed up. This can be no fun. It can be painful; admitting to yourself that there were times when your anger made you abusive, or reliving a past event that made you feel shame, can be one of the hardest things you've ever done. It can feel like you won't survive it. But I promise you it is both necessary and survivable! You will not believe what a relief it is to stare these things down and come out of it freer and happier.

CHAPTER 11:

Possibilities

It's hard to believe right now, when you're in the midst of dealing with an out-of-control teen, but it can become something you are grateful for. If you are anything like me, your greatest lessons and blessings come from your most challenging experiences.

The first of the difficult times for which I ended up being grateful is when my second husband and I separated. My daughter was ten and my son was three years old. It made me realize that I couldn't keep doing things the way I was doing them and feeling the way I was feeling. It was the best worst thing that ever happened to me. It kicked off my healing journey, and I am so thankful.

The most significant of these times were the long, painful years of my son's teenagerhood. Do I wish they could have been different? Yes. And I wouldn't be who I am today if they hadn't happened. Sometimes the cosmic two-by-four seems a lot bigger than just a two-by-four, and sometimes that's just what I needed.

You've started the process of finding the good in this situation. By learning how to tap, you now have a tool literally at your fingertips to find calm and clarity. By working through some of your story – your limiting beliefs around parenting and yourself – you've opened yourself to new possibilities. By tapping on the shame, fear, guilt, anger, impatience, and more, you've started to uncover who you are without the untruths that had you in their grips.

I encourage you to continue tapping and to be open to what this experience has to offer for learning and growing and healing. Grab the opportunity to release the old, undermining beliefs. Believe in the possibilities of an inner calm, more ease, and a better relationship with your child.

It's possible, I promise!

ACKNOWLEDGMENTS

My biggest thank you goes to my son Jason Nichols and my daughter Sabrina Mejia-Nichols, who gave me permission to include information about them in this book. Thank you for your support, for forgiving me my trespasses, and for being my biggest teachers.

Many thanks to Dr. Angela Lauria and the team at The Author Incubator for your support, your commitment to helping others who want to make a difference, and your butt-kicking. It was just what I needed!

I thank Rob Nelson and Victoria Vines of Tapping the Matrix Academy for shepherding me through my EFT/Matrix Reimprinting certification. I also thank Rob for allowing me to adapt his "write your own script" process.

I am so grateful to Rev. David McArthur and all of my dear friends at Unity of Walnut Creek who supported me through those difficult years in so many ways, who have loved and accepted me just as I am (and challenged me to grow in so many ways), and are now so supportive of me as I write this book and begin a new chapter in my life. There are so many, and I would feel terrible if I left someone out, so know that each one of you is appreciated.

I appreciate my sister Debbie's unconditional support; she is the only one left who shares with me the memories of our childhood. I am grateful for the friendship I have with my Uncle Ron and Aunt Karen; it means a lot to me. Thank you to my sisters-in-law Jann and Wendy. We should go to Tahoe more often (and bring Sharon). Thank you to Natazha Bernie for your friendship and support.

I am extra grateful for my husband John, his never-ending support, and how he always sees the best in me, even when I can't.

I would also like to acknowledge the Morgan James Publishing Team: David Hancock, CEO & Founder; my Author Relations Manager, Bonnie Rauch, and special thanks to Jim Howard, Bethany Marshall, and Nickcole Watkins.

THANK YOU

Thanks so much for reading my book. I wish with all my heart that this book brought peace and hope into your life and some shifts in your relationship with your teenager.

As mentioned in Chapter 4, you can head over to my website for a video tutorial on how to tap. As a thank you gift just for my readers, a bonus chapter and companion videos are available at: www.tappingintoyourtrueself.com/bonus-videos.

I am so grateful and in awe of your commitment to your son or daughter. Thank you for doing so much to support them in this difficult phase of their life.

I salute you for being brave enough and caring enough to support yourself. It doesn't always seem like you have the time or that it makes sense to address your own needs. I believe doing so makes you one smart mama.

With all my best wishes,

Lisa

ABOUT THE AUTHOR

Lisa Nichols is a certified EFT and Matrix Reimprinting practitioner. She specializes in helping moms become the moms they want to be. She founded Tapping Into Your True Self in 2018 and works with clients internationally by phone and Zoom.

Lisa specializes in helping moms find calm amidst the chaos. Tapping can help moms:

- Clear stored emotions and beliefs that add to their stress
- Let go of any unreasonable expectations about themselves or parenting
- Feel less anxious and more hopeful

- Address other issues in their lives – relationships, work, weight, prosperity, etc.

Lisa has an MS in agricultural journalism from the University of Wisconsin Madison (the only time she has lived outside of California). She had an assortment of roles before she found her passion with EFT, among them as a reporter for a fresh produce industry newspaper, vice president at a large national bank, personal assistant for a children's book author, and operations manager for a nonprofit – all while being a mom. In 2007, she and her family started a lawn greeting business that she continues to run today and for which her son plays a key role: delivering the flocks of flamingos and other ornaments.

Lisa has been an overachieving volunteer in schools, Scouts and her spiritual community, Unity of Walnut Creek, where she has served on the Board of Trustees for ten years. It is at Unity where she started her journey of personal growth and healing; it was also the first place she experienced tapping.

Lisa currently resides in Concord, California, with her husband, daughter, and three adorable cats. She loves supporting causes she believes in, hosting parties for her husband's winery and as fundraisers, playing pool while watching the Warriors win, and international travel.

Website: www.tappingintoyourtrueself.com

Email: hello@tappingintoyourtrueself.com

Facebook: www.facebook.com/tappingintoyourtrueself

CPSIA information can be obtained
at www.ICGtesting.com
Printed in the USA
JSHW021410280222
23432JS00001B/35